LONGMAN HISTORY PROJECT

South Africa 1948–2000: the Rise and Fall of Apartheid

Third Edition

MARTIN ROBERTS

General Editor: Josh Brooman

Pearson Education Limited
Edinburgh Gate
Harlow
Essex CM20 2JE
England
and Associated Companies throughout the world

First published 1996
Second Edition 2001
Third Edition 2001
Sixth impression 2007

ISBN 978-0-582-47383-6

The right of Martin Roberts to be identified as author of this work has been asserted by him in accordance with the Copyright, Designs and Patents Act 1988.

Set in Concorde and Tekton

First edition produced by Hart McLeod

Printed in China
GCC/06

The Publisher's policy is to use paper manufactured from sustainable forests.

Illustrations by Sheila Betts

Cover photograph: Popperfoto

Acknowledgements

We are grateful to the following for permission to reproduce photographs and other copyright material:

Associated Newspapers Group Ltd, page 46; The Associated Press Ltd, page 54 (below), 79, 98, 102, 111 (above), The Associated Press/John Parkin, page 94; Steve Biko '*I Write What I Like*', Penguin Books, 1988 (photo by Aelred Stubbs), page 81; Camera Press Ltd, pages 65, 74, 78, 107, Camera Press/IDAF, page 82; *Daily Graphic*, June 1902, page 18; *Die Burger*, page 92; *The Guardian*, 19.6.92, page 117 (above left); Hulton Deutsch Collection, page 38; Helen Joseph, '*Side by Side*', Zed Books Ltd, 1986, page 36; Joseph Harker, *The Legacy of Apartheid, The Guardian* 1994 (photo by Clem Elmendorp), page 47; Link Picture Library, page 14, 30 (right), Orde Eliason/Link, page 73, Greg English/Link, pages 72, 97 (above right); Little Brown & Co UK for extracts from *Long Walk to Freedom* by Nelson Mandela pages 44, 68, 112, 113, 121, 122; Mansell Collection page 17; The Mayibuye Centre, University of the Western Cape, South Africa, pages 21, 22, 23, 31, 34, 43, 44, 48, 71, 83, 84, 86, 91, 97 (below left), 108, 110, 111 (below), Museum Africa, Johannesburg, pages 6, 7, 8, 10; *Natal Mercury*, 28.5.48, page 24; National Cultural Museum, Pretoria, page 25; National Monuments Council, South Africa, page 11; 'PA' News, page 54 (above); Popperfoto, pages 4, 5, 39, 42, 113 (below left), 115, 119, 120, 121; Rex Features/SIPA, page 101 (left); *South Africa Since 1948*, Wayland Publishers, page 95; *South Africa Sunday Times*, 3.10.65, page 57; *Southern Africa Business News*, Oct/Nov. 1986, page 101 (right); Jogo Silva/Southlight Photo Agency, South Africa, page 116, Paul Velasco/Southlight, page 117 (below right); *The Sowetan*, 31.3.89, page 103; WT Stead, 'Review of Reviews', pages 15; Topham/AP, page 113 (above right), Topham Picturepoint, pages 13, 26, 64, 93; PA Photos, page 134 top (European Photo Agency); Popperfoto/Reuter, page 126; The South African Sunday Times, 9 July 2000, page 132; text abridged from *www.suntimes.co.za/2000/07/09*; Frank Spooner Pictures/Johann Van Tonder, page 134 bottom; Topham Picturepoint/ImageWorks, page 127; Zapiro, Sowetan, 17 February 1999, page 131.

We have been unable to trace the copyright holders for the material on the following pages, and would be grateful for any information that would enable us to do so: 15, 30 (left), 36, 47, 49, 81, 95.

Picture Research by Sandie Huskinson-Rolfe (PHOTOSEEKERS)

Contents

Introduction

Source 1

The British royal family on a tour of South Africa in 1947, with the South African Prime Minister, Jan Smuts (wearing a white hat).

In 1947 the British royal family made a tour of South Africa. The tour was a great success. King George VI was proud to visit South Africa, which was part of the British Commonwealth. More than 300,000 South Africans, white and black, had fought courageously with the Allies during the Second World War. Their Prime Minister, Jan Smuts, was a famous international statesman who had played a leading part in setting up the League of Nations in 1919 and in writing the charter of the United Nations in 1945.

Smuts, although a champion of democracy and liberty overseas, at home believed firmly in segregation – which meant separating black people from white – and in preventing blacks from having political rights.

In 1947 such policies did not greatly worry British or white international opinion. Through their vast overseas empires, Europeans controlled almost all of Africa and much of the rest of the world. Segregation was common in the United States. White supremacy still seemed normal.

In the next twenty years, world opinion changed completely. The European empires collapsed and with them much of the racist thinking that whites were superior. The US government outlawed segregation. But white South Africa would not change. On the contrary, the National Party which defeated Smuts in the 1948 general election set the country on an even more white supremacist and racist path. South Africa became an 'apartheid state', meaning that black people were separated from white people in every imaginable way.

In 1947 Nelson Mandela was 28 and studying for a law degree. He was also a rising star in the African National Congress (ANC), the oldest and largest black political movement in South Africa.

The ANC had little time for Smuts since, in 1943, when it had put its case for full democratic rights for blacks in a pamphlet called 'African Claims', he had dismissed it without even a discussion. Young black leaders like Mandela, Walter Sisulu and Oliver Tambo realised that they would only gain their freedom by actions stronger than writing pamphlets and that it would not be easily won. Never, however, in even their most depressed moments, did they think that fifty more years would have to pass before real democracy would come to their country; that they themselves would spend thirty years in prison or exile; and that white governments would murder thousands of their supporters and imprison many more.

The next royal visit took place in 1995 (see Source 2). It seemed a near miracle to many people that Mandela had been elected as President of a multi-racial South Africa the year before; equally miraculous seemed the readiness of the victorious ANC to reassure white South Africans that their place in the new nation was secure, despite the terrible things their governments had done to blacks over the years.

The purpose of this book is to describe this extraordinary period in South Africa's history and to explain the rise and fall of the white-controlled apartheid state.

Source 2

Nelson Mandela receives the Order of Merit from Queen Elizabeth II in 1995.

Part 1: Race relations in South Africa up to 1948
Unit 1 · Historical background

The early inhabitants

In the 1946 census, the total population of South Africa was 11,415,945. Sixty-nine per cent were classed as African, 21 per cent as White, 8 per cent as Coloured and 2 per cent as Asian. How had this racial mixture happened? To find the answer, we have to start by looking at South Africa's earliest inhabitants, the Khoisan.

The Khoisan

The brown-skinned Khoisan had occupied southern Africa for at least 2,000 years. They can be divided into two groups: the San, who lived mainly by hunting and whom the first whites called 'Bushmen' (Source 1); and the Khoikhoi, who herded cattle and whom the whites called 'Hottentots'.

Black Bantu-speaking farmers

By AD 1600 there were probably about 120,000 Khoisan living mainly in the south and west of the country. Meanwhile, from about AD 400, iron-using Bantu-speaking black farmers were settling in the best-watered areas of the north and east. They herded cattle, sheep and goats and cultivated grain crops. They grouped themselves in tribes or clans of varying sizes, each led by a chief, and moved when pastures failed or enemies threatened. They greatly outnumbered the Khoisan, there being 3.5 million of them in the 1904 census.

Source 1

San hunters armed for an expedition. A painting by Samuel Daniell, about 1830.

Source 2

'The Cabo de Goede Hoop' (Cape of Good Hope) drawn by the Dutchman Abraham Bogaert in 1706. Note the Khoikhoi settlement in the foreground and the white settlement across the bay.

Conflict between the races

San rock paintings show Khoisan and blacks fighting fiercely for cattle. The blacks usually won, being physically stronger as well as more numerous and better armed. As the blacks took over the more fertile land, the Khoisan either retreated westwards or became the herdsmen-servants of their black conquerors.

The Portuguese

In the fifteenth century Europeans began to trade across the world. For the next 500 years they controlled much of this trade. At first their main interest was 'the Indies' (India and the Far East), and they only came across southern Africa as it turned out to be on the main sea route to the Indies. From 1488 the Portuguese were the first to explore the coast and then press on to the Indies, but they did not settle.

The Dutch establish a base at Cape Town, 1652

For the next 150 years European ships swung round the Cape but few stopped there since the coast was dangerous. Things changed when the Dutch East India Company decided to establish a base beside Table Bay near the southern tip of Africa. It wanted to supply its Indies fleet with fresh food and water. Jan van Riebeeck set up that base successfully in 1652, in effect founding the port of Cape Town (see Source 2).

The whites and the Khoikhoi

Soon there was trouble between the Dutch and the Khoikhoi. Van Riebeeck allowed some Dutch to farm near the company's base. What the Khoikhoi saw was whites taking lands which had always been theirs to graze, and they responded by raiding the Dutch herds.

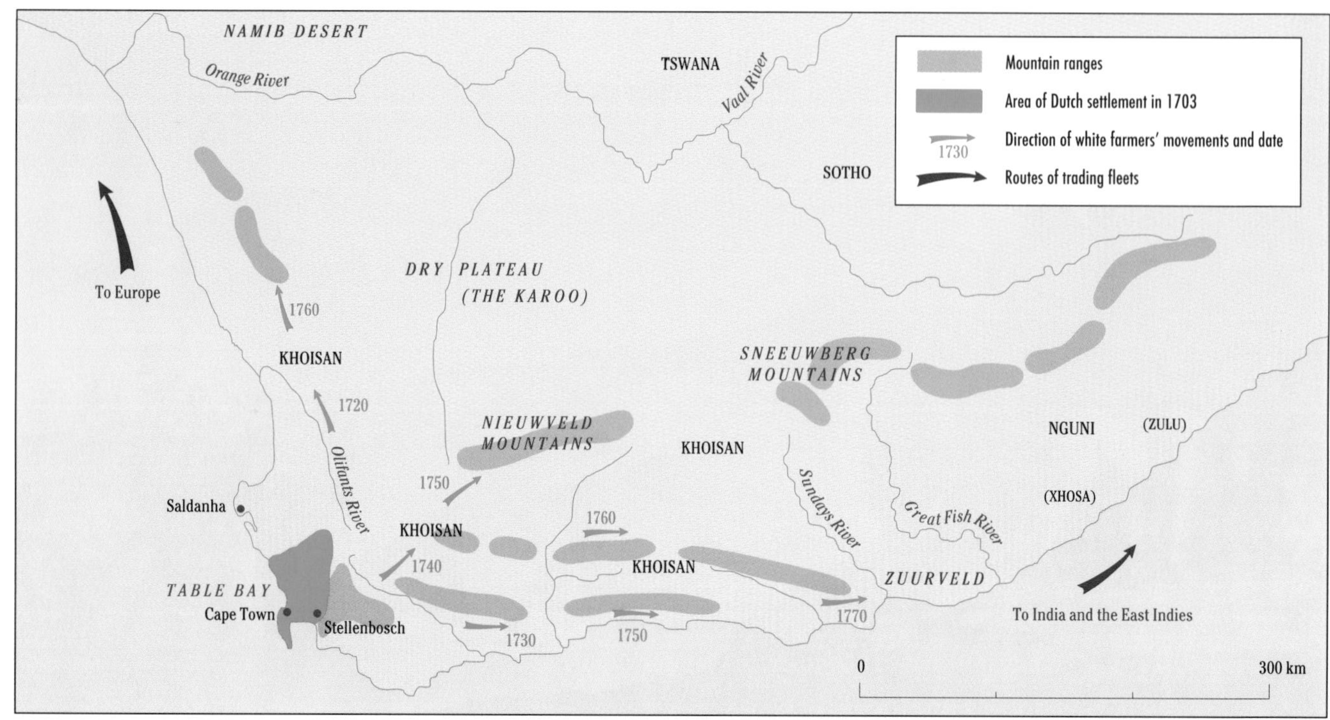

Source 3

South Africa's early settlements, 1652–1770.

In the wars which followed, the Dutch were easily victorious with their much superior weapons, and Van Riebeeck took possession of the Cape in 1659.

Then European diseases like smallpox wiped out most Khoikhoi, killing nine out of ten by 1770.

The white settlement continued to grow as Germans and French as well as Dutch arrived, mainly to farm cattle. By 1780 they numbered more than 10,000 and had fanned out with their herds from Cape Town (see Source 3). The Khoikhoi became their servants and the Dutch East India Company shipped in slaves from the Far East, which further added to the sense of white superiority.

As for the San, the whites treated them hardly better than wild animals. They hunted them down (see Source 4), killing the adults and capturing the children to work on their farms.

Source 4

Boers (Dutch farmers) hunting San raiders who had taken their cattle, painted in about 1820 by C.D. Bell.

The Cape Coloured

In the early years of the Dutch settlement, white men frequently had sex with Khoikhoi women. The result was children of mixed parentage, who became known as Cape Coloured. However, white Cape society was strongly racist. A French traveller in the Cape in 1783 talked with a Cape Coloured woman who told him of:

Source 5

Le Vaillant, *Journey to the African Interior*, 1790.

> the great contempt which the whites have for the blacks and those of mixed parentage such as myself. To settle myself among them was to expose myself to daily disgrace and insults.

White and black farmers meet

White farmers reached the Zuurveld (see Source 3) in the 1770s. Here they met black farmers for the first time in the shape of the Xhosa people. The Zuurveld was good grazing land, but its mixture of sweet and sour grasses forced herds to move according to the seasons. Arguments between blacks and whites became frequent, and the first open war took place in 1779.

The Xhosa proved a tougher enemy than the Khoisan. They were better led, better armed and more numerous. Nor did they die from European diseases in the same way. This last fact is crucial to South African history. In many other parts of the world – for example, North America and Australia – whites not only defeated the native inhabitants but also came to outnumber them because the diseases they imported proved to be killers. This did not happen to black South Africans. In 1770, they were already much the largest racial group and have remained so ever since.

Questions

1 Study Sources 1, 2 and 4. What do they tell you about the San and the Khoikhoi?

2 Read page 6 and study Source 3.
a Who else inhabited southern Africa before the arrival of the whites?
b Where mainly did they settle?
c How did they get on with the Khoisan?

3 Read pages 7–9.
a Why did whites first settle in the Cape?
b How did they treat the Khoisan?

4 How and when did the whites first come into conflict with the blacks?

5 Using the information on pages 7–9, make a list of reasons why the various races in southern Africa fought one another.

The British arrive

In 1800 Britain was the strongest industrial and naval power in the world and, during the nineteenth century, created the largest empire in history. The heart of this empire was India. In 1815, to protect the sea route to India, Britain took the Cape from the Dutch (see Source 2).

Source 1

Shaka Zulu, from a sketch by a British army officer in 1825.

How did the British affect the other peoples?

The Xhosa now found themselves up against a different enemy. The Dutch farmers never had a strong army behind them. In contrast, the British could ship in as many troops as they needed from other parts of the Empire. They drove the Xhosa back beyond the Kei River (see Source 2). In the 1830s white farmers found that the Eastern Cape well suited the merino, a fine wool-producing sheep. Wool, grown mainly for British textile factories, quickly became the Cape's most important export. A network of white-controlled farms and villages europeanised the interior.

The Difaqane (scattering of peoples)

Meanwhile, further to the north-east, Shaka, a brilliant military leader (see Source 1), let loose his Zulu regiments against his neighbours. By 1824 he was master of a wide area around the Tugela and Pongola rivers (see Source 2).

Shaka was murdered in 1828, but the effects of his wars spread widely to the west and north. Different peoples – such as the Ngwane, Hlubi, Tlokwa and the Ndebele – fled from the Zulus into the interior where they

Source 2

The Eastern Cape, the Difaqane and the Great Trek.

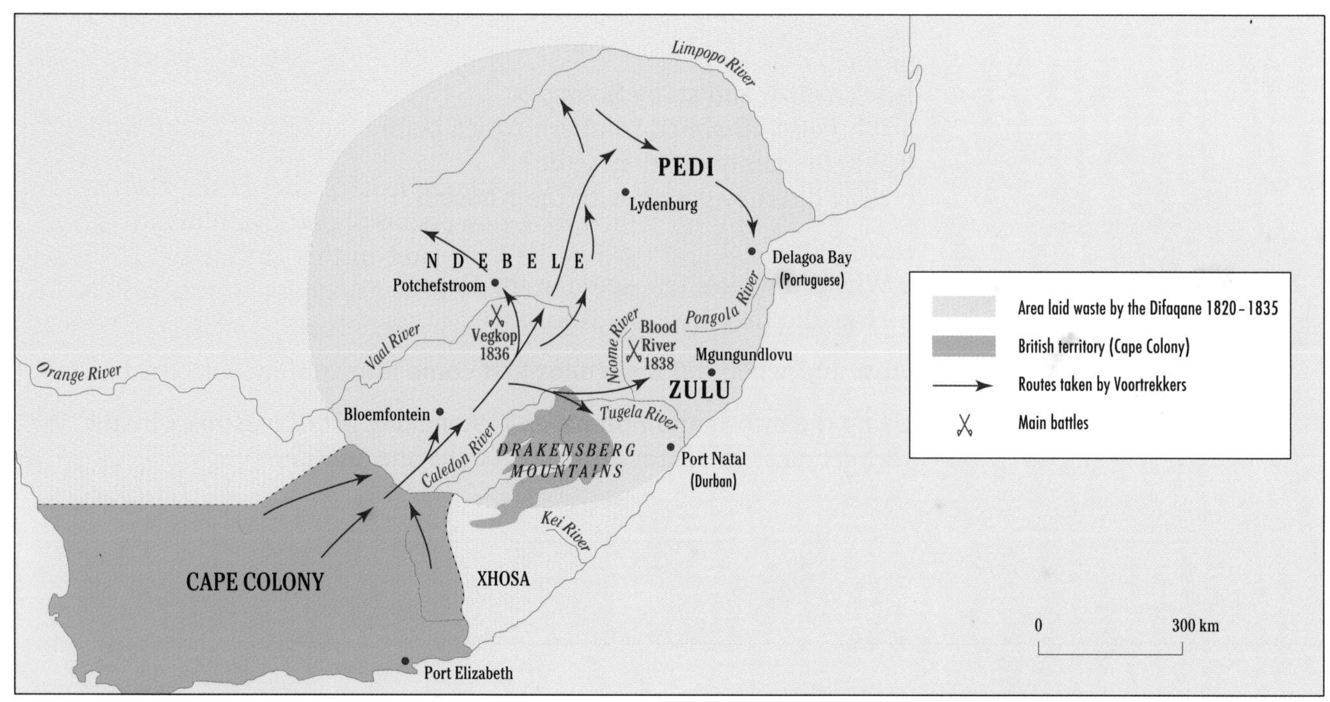

fought among themselves for new lands on which to settle. The results of this 'scattering of peoples' were destruction, starvation and death on a large scale. Parts of the plateau and eastern coastlands were left virtually empty of people, and the surviving chiefs of all the peoples except the Zulus were much weaker.

The Voortrekkers (the people who travelled away)
In the Cape, the British found the Khoikhoi being strictly controlled by the whites. The 'Hottentot Codes' forced Khoikhoi adults and children to carry passes in order to work on white farms. Outspoken British missionaries like Dr John Philip strongly criticised such regulations, and within Britain attitudes turned against slavery. The Cape government abolished the Hottentot Codes in 1828, the British government slavery in 1833. For many Boers this was too much. They believed that the over-interfering British threatened their whole way of life. Between 1835 and 1845, 14,000 Boers, with the same number of Khoikhoi and black servants, left Cape Colony. Their main aim was, in the words of one of their leaders, Piet Retief:

Source 3
W.A. de Klerk, *The Puritans in Africa*, 1975.

to maintain such regulations as may suppress crime ... to preserve proper relationships between master and servant ... and to lead a more quiet life than we have heretofore done.

Source 2 shows how the Voortrekkers travelled into the areas emptied by the Difaqane. Their most dangerous enemies on the plateau were the Ndebele people, whom they held off at the battle of Vegkop (1836) and then drove away with the help of some black allies. When Retief with his group of trekkers tried to settle among the Zulus, Dingane, Shaka's successor, had them murdered. Five hundred Boers, led by Andries Pretorius, avenged this murder on 16 December 1838 beside the Ncome (later called Blood River). There, with their wagons in a 'laager' or circle, they defeated 10,000 Zulus, killing 3,000 of them, without loss of life to themselves. They then took possession of part of Zululand.

We shall see later in this Unit (page 25) how in the 1930s Boer (Afrikaner) historians and politicians turned the events of 1838 into a nationalist and racist myth. Retief's murder became an act of black savagery, and the 'miraculous' victory at Blood River a sign that the Voortrekkers and their descendants were God's people who alone had the right to rule South Africa. Source 4 is an example of how the myth was created.

Source 4
The bronze wagon memorial at Blood River. This life-size monument is a good example of Afrikaner nationalist thinking.

The British, however, were not having unfriendly Boers close to Durban, the only good harbour in South Africa apart from Cape Town. The British navy arrived in Durban in 1842, and most Boers trekked once more into the interior rather than again accept British rule.

Consequently, by 1850 the British had two coastal colonies – Cape Colony and Natal – and the Boers had created two independent states in the interior – the Orange Free State and the South African Republic (the Transvaal). Some black peoples, notably the Zulus and the Pedi, still kept some of their old independence.

Questions

1 **a** Re-read pages 10-12. Why did the British come to South Africa, and which two colonies did they rule there in 1850?
b What effect did their arrival have on the Xhosa?

2 Study Sources 1 and 2.
a Who was Shaka?
b Why did his actions lead to a 'scattering of peoples'?
c How did this black-against-black violence help the Voortrekkers?

3 Study Sources 2, 3 and 4.
a Who were the Voortrekkers and why did they dislike British rule?
b What happened to Piet Retief?
c Why did an Afrikaner government in the twentieth century put up such a monument at Blood River?
d What had the Voortrekkers gained by 1850?

Diamonds and gold

Rich diamond fields were found in South Africa in 1867. In 1886 gold-fields were also discovered. Mines were quickly dug. These diamond and gold mines greatly changed South Africa. They created wealth, cities and new kinds of employment. They made the British determined to take control of all South Africa.

How did these discoveries affect the peoples of South Africa?

Diamonds

Within ten years of the discovery of the first diamonds, £60 million of the stones had been sold and Kimberley, the diamond town with 30,000 inhabitants, had become the country's second city after Cape Town.

At first miners worked on 'claims' only 3.7m^2 (see Source 1). The deeper the mine, the more dangerous the mining and the greater the problem of flooding. Clever businessmen purchased water pumps and bought

Source 1 The 'Big Hole', Kimberley. The miners are digging down into the diamond-bearing 'blue ground' soil. This is drawn to the surface in buckets along the steel ropes.

out other miners. Two men soon dominated the diamond scene, Cecil Rhodes and Barney Barnato. In 1888, Rhodes bought out Barnato and secured a monopoly of diamond production in South Africa.

Gold

Prospectors found what proved to be the richest gold mines in the world on the Witwatersrand (Rand) in 1886. Since the gold was spread in thin seams very deep underground, big money was needed to pay for its extraction. That soon came from diamond profits and from European investors. By 1895, 10,000 whites and 100,000 blacks worked in seventy-nine mines, and by 1913 South Africa produced 40 per cent of the world's gold. Johannesburg, centre of the industry with 250,000 inhabitants, had, in twenty-five years, grown from nothing into South Africa's largest city.

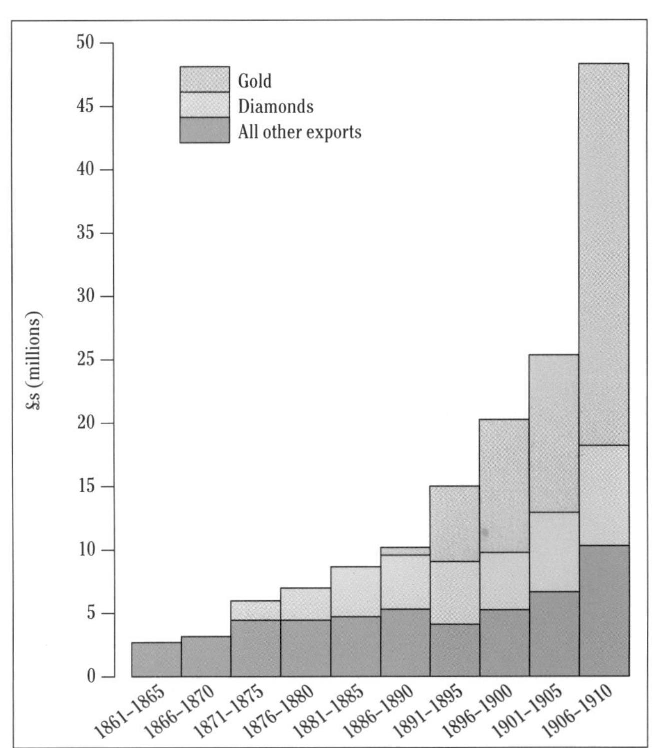

Source 2 Exports from South Africa, 1861–1910.

Migrant labour and compounds

In both the diamond and gold mines, black men did most of the hard physical labour. They usually worked on short contracts, migrating to and from their rural villages. Since diamonds are easily stolen, the diamond companies strictly supervised their workers in male-only compounds. The gold-mining companies used the same system, so black migrant workers, housed in large, male-only compounds, became an important feature of twentieth-century South African life.

The mining companies liked the migrant system because it helped them keep down black wages. They justified the low wages by pointing out that they met the basic needs of their workers by housing and feeding them in compounds. They did not worry about how such wages affected the black women and children far away in the countryside.

White governments also liked the migrant system because it helped them keep blacks segregated from whites. The movement of blacks in and out of the mainly white towns was controlled by passes (see Source 3).

So migrant labour looks like a nasty system forced on the blacks by hard-headed and hard-hearted white businessmen. However, things were not so simple, at least to begin with. Many blacks liked the system too. Young men could migrate quite easily to the mines and return home with useful extra earnings. The migrant system became really burdensome when the rural areas became too crowded for families to make a decent living and the government prevented black families settling permanently in towns where the work was.

Source 3

The hated pass was still in force for blacks 80 years after its introduction in 1896.

The sugar industry
In this same period, between 1860 and 1900, British companies successfully established sugar plantations in Natal. Since they could not persuade enough blacks to work on the plantations, they shipped in more than 15,000 Indians to do the work. From this group emerged South Africa's Asian community.

Questions

1 Study Sources 1 and 2 and pages 12 and 13. How and why did the pattern of South African exports change between 1866–70 and 1886–90, and between 1886–90 and 1906–10?

2 Study Source 3 and pages 14 and 15.
a Why did black workers have to carry identity cards?
b Why did white companies and governments like the migrant labour system?

Britain and the Boers

Source 1 Cartoon of the 'Ambitions of Cecil Rhodes' from the 1890s. Note the following: Rhodes striding across Africa; the train on its way from Cape Town to Bulawayo; the line which reaches across Africa to the Nile and Cairo in the north; and, in 'Fort Folly', the Boer leader, Paul Kruger.

In the last quarter of the nineteenth century the nations of Europe took part in an extraordinary display of empire-building. One result of this empire-building or imperialism, was that almost all of Africa came under European control. The British were major players in this 'scramble for Africa'. Where South Africa was concerned, they were determined that they, rather than their European rivals, should get possession of its riches.

Britain already possessed the diamond fields. The gold mines were a different matter since the Rand sat right in the middle of the Boer South African Republic. In an attempt to win Boer support, the British army defeated both the Zulus and Pedi between 1878 and 1881. However, led by Paul Kruger, the Boers refused to be drawn into the British Empire. On the contrary, they defeated a British force at Majuba in 1881.

Why did the Boers and the British become enemies?

Cecil Rhodes

Rhodes was the most imperialist of all British imperialists. As a young man he had made a fortune in diamonds. He became Prime Minister of Cape Colony in 1890. He believed that his mission was to make as much as possible of Africa British. His special ambition was to have a railway built from the Cape to Cairo which passed only through British colonies (see Source 1). Between 1890 and 1896 his private company seized the lands between the Limpopo and the Zambezi and called them 'Rhodesia' in his honour.

The Jameson Raid

Rhodes' main target was the Rand gold-fields but here his efforts ended in failure. He supported his friend Dr Jameson who led a raid into the South African Republic (the Transvaal) in 1895 in the hope that the British mining people would rise in revolt and overthrow its government. They did not, and Boer forces surrounded Jameson and forced him to surrender. Rhodes himself had to resign as Prime Minister of Cape Colony.

The Boer War, 1899–1902

The British, however, did not give up. In 1899, Lord Milner, the senior British official in the Cape, provoked the Boer republics to war. To the world's surprise the tiny Boer armies won some early spectacular victories, but within a year the reinforced British forces had won the decisive battle at Paardeberg and captured the Boer capitals of Bloemfontein and Pretoria.

Source 2

The Anglo-Boer War, 1899–1902.

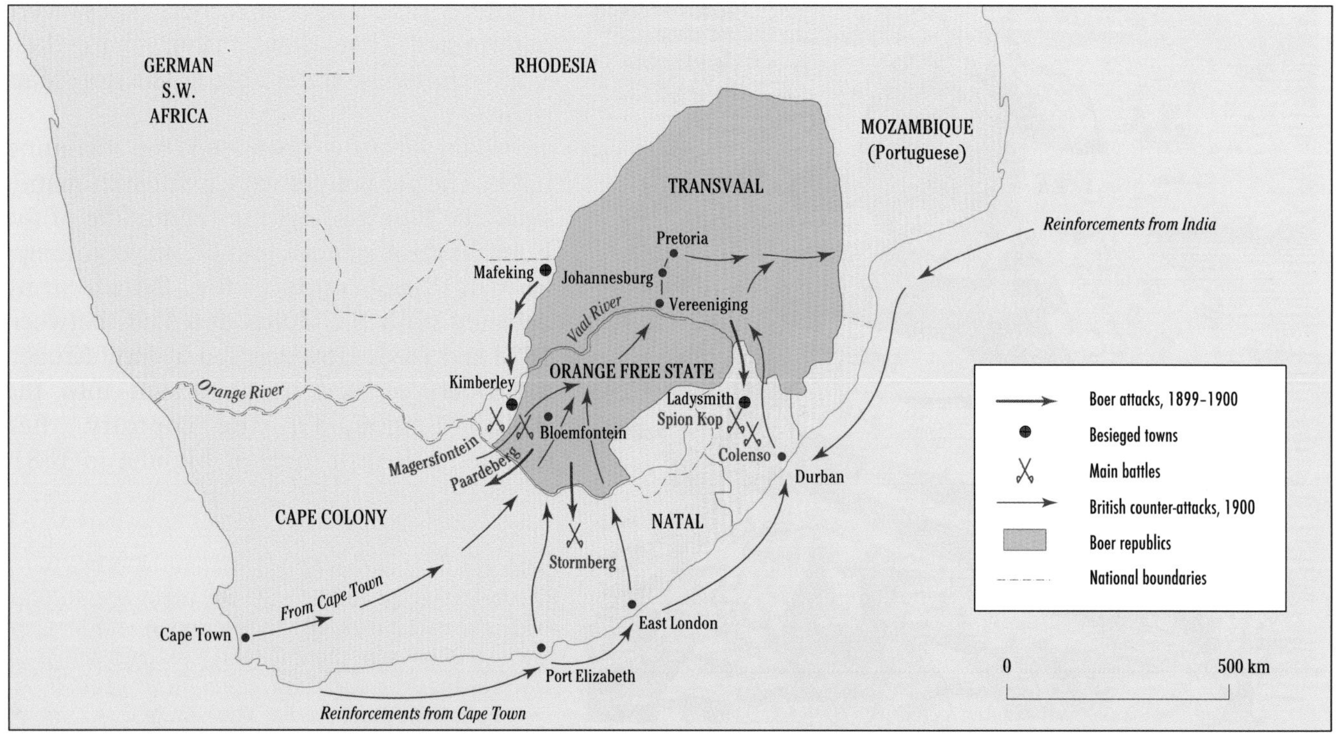

Source 3

A French comment on the concentration camps. Kitchener is shown as a monstrous toad. The caption reads, quoting Kitchener: 'The concentration camps where I have united women and children are speedily doing their work of bringing peace.'

Yet the war continued for two more cruel years. Boer guerrillas raided across the plateau. The British commander, Kitchener, responded by criss-crossing the countryside with barbed wire and by moving Boer women and children into 'concentration camps' so that they could not shelter their menfolk.

The concentration camps were a disaster, their poor sanitation causing the deaths from disease of 28,000 Boer women and children and many thousands of blacks. Finally and bitterly, in 1902, the Boers surrendered. Their two republics, with the gold-fields, became part of the British Empire.

The war was over but at a cost greater even than the thousands of dead and wounded. Most Boers believed that they were the victims of a monstrous British injustice. As far as Henning Klopper, a survivor of the concentration camps and a future Afrikaner leader, was concerned, the only conclusion he could draw from the war was that:

> Milner and Kitchener were out to break the backbone of the Afrikaner and their back-bone consisted of their womenfolk.

Source 4 Henning Klopper, speaking in an interview with BBC reporter David Harrison, in 1981.

For many Afrikaner leaders of the early twentieth century their great ambition was to right these wrongs by making sure that South Africa was an Afrikaner country, not a British one.

Questions

1 Study Source 1 and pages 15 and 16.
- **a** What was 'the scramble for Africa'?
- **b** Describe the part played in it by Cecil Rhodes.
- **c** Do you think the artist approved or disapproved of Rhodes? Explain your answer.
- **d** Explain your own opinions of Rhodes' career.

2 Study Sources 3 and 4 and page 17.
- **a** How badly did the Boers suffer as a result of the Anglo-Boer War of 1899–1902?
- **b** What effect did the war have on the thinking of future Afrikaner nationalists about the British in South Africa?

3 Comment on the reliability of Source 4.

Segregation, 1902–48

The years after the Boer War went better than expected for Afrikaners, worse for blacks. Afrikaner politicians increased the segregation between the races.

How did South Africa become more segregated between 1902 and 1948?

Source 1 predicted the future well. Since many Britons felt guilty about the Boer War, they wished to win over their defeated foe and did so by creating a new Union of South Africa. This was an excellent deal for Afrikaners and an appalling one for blacks. It kept the old voting systems of the pre-Boer War days which meant that only a tiny handful of well-off Cape blacks could vote, far too few to have any influence on national law-making. It also meant that, since there were three Afrikaners to every two English-speaking whites, all white governments from 1910 to 1994 were led by Afrikaners.

Source 1

'Peace with Honour'. Note how the artist shows the Boer (with the beard) as a respected figure and does not have a black anywhere in sight.

PEACE WITH HONOUR!

Lord Kitchener to Secretary of State for War.

"PRETORIA, May 31st (11.15 p.m.).

"Negotiations with Boer delegates.

"The document containing terms of surrender was signed here this evening at 10.30 p.m., by all Boer representatives, as well as by Lord Milner and myself."

BUCKINGHAM PALACE, June 1st, 1902.

"The King has received the welcome news of the cessation of hostilities in South Africa with infinite satisfaction, and trusts that peace may be speedily followed by the restoration of prosperity in his new dominions, and that the feelings necessarily engendered by war will give place to the earnest co-operation of all his Majesty's South African subjects in promoting the welfare of their common country."

HOUSE OF LORDS, June 2nd.

"The Earl of Rosebery: I hope I may be allowed in a single sentence to express to his Majesty's Government my hearty, unstinted, and unreserved congratulations on the announcement of peace, which they have been at liberty to make, and to hope that to-day may mark the beginning of a new epoch of peace, prosperity, and commercial development throughout the Empire and South Africa."

(Cheers,)

The 1913 Land Act

The Union government, led by two ex-Boer War generals, Louis Botha and Jan Smuts, soon passed a new law which hit blacks very hard. The 1913 Land Act forbade blacks either to own land (except in the native reserves which made up only 7 per cent of the country), or to practise share-cropping. Many blacks were share-croppers, which meant that they lived on and cultivated part of a white-owned farm and paid a rent calculated as a share of their crops. In the long term, the Land Act simply turned blacks into labourers for white farmers; in the short term it led to harsh suffering as black share-croppers were evicted.

Sol Plaatje, a black journalist, wrote a vivid account of the effects of the Land Act in his book *Native Life in South Africa*. In it he describes the plight of the Kgobadi family. Both Kgobadi and his father-in-law were evicted share-croppers:

Source 2

Sol Plaatje, *Native Life in South Africa*, 1916.

They were wandering around the roads in the cold winter with everything they owned.... Mrs Kgobadi's child was sick. She had to be put in the ox-wagon which bumped along the road.... Two days later the child died.... Late that night the poor young mother and father had to dig a grave where no-one could see them. They had to bury their child in a stolen grave.

The 1930s: segregation spreads

A Native Economic Commission set up by the government in 1932 justified segregation along these lines: blacks were racially different from whites; they were a rural people, best grouped in tribes and led by chiefs; they were not suited to city life. The commission stated that the best way forward for the country was for blacks to stay in the reserves, which should become more productive through modern farming methods. A new Land Act of 1936 increased the area of the reserves from 7 per cent to 13.5 per cent. At the same time the government abolished black voting rights in the Cape.

Other segregationist laws increased the colour bar so that the more skilled and better-paid jobs were reserved for whites. The laws put greater controls on the movement of blacks into towns, and encouraged the building of black townships well away from city centres.

Economic trends

The South African economy see-sawed between 1914 and 1948. It did well during the First World War, when South Africa fought alongside Britain. A rising gold price helped both the gold mines and local industry to prosper. Harder times came in the 1920s when Afrikaner farmers were hit by drought and disease. The poorer ones left the land and came to the cities in search of work. General Hertzog, now the Prime Minister, responded to this 'poor white' problem by creating jobs for them at the expense of those for blacks, notably on the railways.

Hard times continued in the early 1930s as a result of the Great Depression of 1929–33. They caused an acute political crisis in 1932, which brought Hertzog and Smuts together in a single 'fusion', or coalition, government. However, from 1934, the economy began to grow again fast, a period of growth which in fact lasted without serious interruption for another forty years. This growth was fuelled by another international rise in the gold price, which helped manufacturing industry. The government used its additional income to help white farmers. The economic growth created a rising demand for jobs, especially in the cities. It pulled the races together, rather than pushing them apart. Whereas only 13 per cent of blacks had lived in cities in 1913, 23 per cent did so in 1946.

Questions

1 Look at Source 1.
a Which sections of the South African population were missing from the picture?
b How reliable is this as evidence of the attitude of the British government towards South Africa in 1902?

Re-read pages 19 and 20.

2 In what ways did the Land Act of 1913 increase segregation in South Africa?

3 What events in 1936 increased segregation still further?

4 How did economic trends between 1914 and 1948 (a) increase and (b) reduce segregation?

Black resistance before 1948

As segregation became more effective and more widespread, black people increasingly organised themselves to resist it. But despite energetic campaigning and talented leadership, their resistance failed to halt the spread of segregation. Why was it not more effective?

Why was black resistance so ineffective before 1948?

Though blacks greatly outnumbered the whites, the weakness of their resistance is not surprising. Never in history had they thought of themselves as a single people. Few were well educated, and they were scattered in thousands of farms and villages or migrating to and from the cities. In contrast, the whites not only owned the farms and businesses which provided black jobs but controlled the army and the police force as well. Whatever differences there may have been among them, the whites were united in their intention of 'keeping the blacks in their place'. It was against this background that black resistance began to develop.

The first black political associations

In the early twentieth century a new group of middle-class blacks was emerging – teachers, lawyers, priests – usually Christians educated at mission schools and sometimes at British or American universities. They began to organise themselves in order to gain more political and social rights. They realised that the Act of Union was likely to create a white Parliament in South Africa hostile to reform. So, in 1912, they formed the first national black association, the South African Native National Congress (SANNC). J. I. Dube was its first president, P. K. Seme its treasurer and Sol Plaatje its secretary. It immediately campaigned against the Land Act and, when it failed to influence the South African Parliament, it sent a delegation to London (see Source 1) in a vain attempt to influence the British Parliament.

Despite these failures the SANNC leaders remained moderate and patient. Before long, they believed, the whites would see the justice of their cause.

Smuts, Hertzog and segregation

They were wrong. Both the Afrikaners who dominated white politics between 1918 and 1948, Smuts and Hertzog, were convinced

Source 1

The SANNC delegation to London, 1914. Rev J.I. Dube is in the centre, Sol Plaatje on the far right.

segregationists. Their main difference lay in their attitudes to the British. Whereas Smuts believed that both white groups should work closely together within the British Empire, Hertzog put Afrikaners first and fiercely opposed Smuts' decision to fight alongside Britain in the Second World War.

The 1920s and 1930s

Generally speaking, the blacks' situation worsened in the 1920s and 1930s. In the reserves, drought and disease made survival more difficult. In the mines, although white wages rose by 10 per cent, black wages fell by the same amount.

This led to an increase in black resistance: the refusal to pay taxes, anti-pass law demonstrations, and strikes such as the 1920 miners' strike which the government crushed with its troops. Another less direct form of protest was the abandoning of the long-established white churches for much more African forms of Christianity.

Source 2

The cover of *Africans' Claims*, published by the ANC in 1943. This was the demand for full democratic rights which Smuts rejected in 1944 (see page 5).

Congress Series No. II.

AFRICANS' CLAIMS

IN SOUTH AFRICA.

Issued and Published by the African National Congress, Rosenberg Arcade, 58, Market Street, Johannesburg, and Printed by the Liberty Printers, 325, 6th Sreet, Asiatic Bazaar, Pretoria.

The most important political movement was the Industrial and Commercial Workers' Union (ICU) which, between 1926 and 1928, Clements Kadalie turned from a Cape Town trade union into a mass protest movement involving both urban and rural blacks. At its height it may have had 100,000 members but quarrels among its leaders led to its collapse.

The SANNC, which changed its name to the ANC (African National Congress) in 1923, kept going. It sent another delegation to Britain in 1919, again in the vain hope of gaining better black rights. Most of its leaders continued to be respectable middle-class men who were unhappy with mass demonstration and suspicious of the socialist and communist ideas which other blacks were finding attractive. The Communist Party of South Africa (CPSA) was founded in 1921. It had a stormy relationship with Kadalie, who expelled its members from the ICU.

The Second World War

The war accelerated many of the trends of the 1930s. Mining and manufacturing boomed, providing more jobs in the cities. Worsening conditions in the rural areas caused a surge of blacks towards the cities. Wartime pressures caused Smuts to relax both the colour bar and the enforcement of the pass laws.

The revival of the ANC

Dr A. B. Xuma, who became President of the ANC in 1940, rescued a struggling organisation. In 1944 he reorganised it, put its finances on to a secure footing and attracted some able young new members who formed its Youth League. The most outstanding were Anton Lembede, Walter Sisulu, Nelson Mandela and Oliver Tambo.

Anton Lembede was a brilliant young schoolteacher from a poor peasant background who died in 1947 when he was only 33. He was the driving force of the Youth League, by which he aimed to give new life to the ANC and 'build up the spirit of African Nationalism throughout South Africa'.

Walter Sisulu was also from peasant stock and largely self-educated. He had worked in the mines and was an active trade unionist. A man of few words and with a hot temper, he was, however, an excellent organiser.

Nelson Mandela (see Source 3) was the son of a chief and educated at mission school and Fort Hare University. Though he too had worked in the mines, his aim was to be a lawyer. A tall, impressive man with a commanding personality, he had a strong sense of which political actions were likely to be effective.

Oliver Tambo too had had a good education and attended Fort Hare, though he came from a peasant family. He was a teacher before joining Mandela to set up a legal practice. Quiet and thoughtful, he was another excellent organiser.

By 1948, thanks mainly to the Youth League, the ANC was ready to give more effective leadership to black resistance than ever before.

The new Afrikaner nationalism of the 1930s

At the same time, however, a stronger, even more racist nationalism had developed among Afrikaners. Daniel Malan with nineteen other MPs had split off from Hertzog's National Party (NP) when Hertzog and Smuts joined forces in 1934. Malan, born in 1874, had been a minister in the Dutch Reformed Church and a newspaper editor before becoming an MP. He formed the Purified National Party, which had a vision of an Afrikaner 'volk' or people who, united by trek (see page 11), racial threat and war against Britain, had a mission to safeguard Christian civilisation in South Africa.

Malan skilfully won the support of the Dutch Reformed Church (the main Afrikaner church) and also of the Broederbond, a secret society of the most influential Afrikaner men. Its aim was, in the words of its chairman, Professor J. C. van Rooy, identical to Malan's: 'a completely independent genuine Afrikaans government for South Africa'.

Source 3

Yusuf Dadoo, president of the South African Indian Congress, speaks to a protest meeting in Johannesburg in 1945. Nelson Mandela, representing the ANC Youth League, is behind the microphone.

The effects of the Second World War on white party politics

The party which Hertzog and Smuts had formed in 1934 was called the United Party (UP). During the 1930s it held the support of most whites, Afrikaner as well as English.

Hertzog believed South Africa should not support Britain in the Second World War. Smuts believed it should. So they split. As Source 4 shows, this split pushed Hertzog towards Malan and made the UP more dependent on English support. Malan strongly opposed South Africa's support for the Allies. Some extremist Afrikaners wanted a German victory and tried to weaken the war effort by sabotage.

In the election of 1943, which Smuts called when it became clear that the tide of war was turning against Hitler, the UP gained an apparently convincing victory. It won eighty-nine seats, more than double the forty-three of Malan's NP. However, while the smaller parties lost seats to the UP, the NP gained two and was able to provide increasingly effective opposition to Smuts.

Source 4

The Second World War caused a split in 1939 between Smuts and Hertzog, who left the United Party and rejoined the Nationalists. Here the Cartoonist Boonzaier shows Smuts taking the Empire road towards European war, while Malan and Hertzog follow the sun-lit South African road.

1943–48: what went wrong for Smuts?

1943–48 proved difficult years for the UP. On the one hand, it faced the more confident opposition of the ANC, which pointed out that the freedom for which South African troops were fighting in Europe was no different from the freedom which they were demanding for all South Africans. On the other, it faced the very different but equally confident opposition of the NP, which was totally opposed to giving any political rights to the black majority. As more and more blacks moved into the towns and the booming war economy led to the weakening of the colour bar in the job market, Malan played on the white fears of being overwhelmed by the black tide.

In 1945 Smuts was seventy-five and was losing his political touch. He did not understand the rising generation of Afrikaners. He angered the large Indian community in the province of Natal by stopping them buying land in previously 'white' areas. As for the blacks, he had no idea what would be the best way forward.

Smuts' thinking about race relations

For most of his life Smuts did not believe that the blacks should mingle with whites or have similar political rights:

Source 5

Jan Smuts speaking at the Imperial Institute, London, in 1917.

... in land ownership and forms of government we are trying to keep them (blacks and whites) apart, and in that way laying down in outline a general policy which it may take a hundred years to work out, but which in the end may be the solution to our native problem. Thus in South Africa you will have in the long run large areas cultivated by blacks and governed by blacks, while in suitable parts you will have your European communities, which will govern themselves separately....

However, as time passed, he grew less confident that separating the races would work.

Source 6

Jan Smuts speaking to the Institute of Race Relations, Cape Town, in 1942.

The high hopes which we had of 'segregation' as a policy have been sadly disappointed.... A revolutionary change is taking place among the native peoples of South Africa through the movement from the country to the towns.... Segregation tried to stop it. It has however not stopped in the least. The process has accelerated. You might as well try to sweep the ocean back with a broom.

But, although he saw the problem and realised that the blacks had a case, he did not dare seek a solution, since he knew that most whites would be hostile to a better political deal for the blacks. Consequently, he never let the leaders of the ANC know that he thought that they had a case. On the contrary, he ignored their campaign against the hated pass laws (see page 14) and used the police and army to crush a miners' strike in 1946. Six miners were killed and 400 injured.

The Fagan and Sauer Reports, 1948

With the 1948 election coming closer, Smuts set up the Fagan Committee to look into the problems being caused by the movement of the blacks into towns. Not to be outdone, Malan appointed his own committee, the Sauer Committee. Both committees published their reports eight weeks before the election. They were very different.

The Fagan Report became the policy of the UP. It argued that total segregation would never work because modern industry and commerce needed a black population permanently and contentedly living in towns close to their workplaces. Migrant labour (see page 14) should be discouraged and black families encouraged to make their homes in well-planned and carefully controlled townships. There was no way they could return to the 'native' reserves which were already overcrowded.

In contrast, the Sauer Report, which became the policy of the NP, argued that the flood of black migrants had to be reversed. 'Apartheid' (separateness) was the only way forward for South Africa. Equality and mixing would mean the suicide of the white race. The reserves must continue to be the real home of the blacks. The migrant labour system must continue and be held in place by the pass laws. Those blacks who had to live in the towns should be treated as temporary visitors without political rights and their numbers strictly controlled.

The 1948 election

THE NATAL MERCURY, FRIDAY, MAY 28, 1948.

SMUTS MAY RESIGN TODAY

Nats. Gain Clear Majority

DR. D. F. MALAN AS NEW PREMIER ?

Platteland Landslide

THE Nationalist-Afrikaner Coalition swept the rural seats in the General Election.

With probably 78 or 79 seats they will be the biggest Party in the new House of Assembly.

GENERAL SMUTS, THE PRIME MINISTER AND LEADER OF THE UNITED PARTY, WAS

LATEST RESULTS

Position Of The Parties At A Glance

SIX OFFER SEATS

British And U.S. Reach Agreement On Palestine

ISRAEL: TRUMAN DENIAL

Source 7
The *Natal Mercury* reports the 1948 general election results.

To the surprise of the world and of Smuts himself, Malan defeated him. The NP with its supporters won seventy-nine seats, the UP and its supporters seventy-one. It was a momentous victory, since the NP was to stay in power for the next forty-six years and, through its apartheid policies, oppress the black majority throughout that period.

The NP won for a number of reasons:

- The electoral system worked in its favour. Though it only gained 40 per cent of the votes against the UP's 50 per cent, it won most of the smaller rural seats while thousands of UP votes were wasted in large urban majorities.
- It played on white fears of the black surge into towns. It said that the Fagan Report placed in danger civilised town life and that Smuts, and particularly Hofmeyr his deputy, were too soft on the blacks and would lead the country to destruction.
- Afrikaners outnumbered the English by a ratio of 3:2. They were on average less rich than the English and more threatened by black labour. Malan managed to secure most of the Afrikaner vote.

To what extent was the 1948 election a turning-point?

Clearly the 1948 election was a turning-point in that it brought to power a new government with particularly racist policies. This government was to stay in power, increasingly out of step with world opinion, for more than forty years. Also new was the confidence this government had in its policies and its ruthlessness in carrying them out.

On the other hand, even if Smuts and Hofmeyr had won and attempted to put into effect policies more favourable to the black majority in political and economic matters, there is little evidence to suggest that they would have carried their party and white opinion with them. Apartheid contained few really new policies. It made the old segregation laws more systematic. It also made impossible the political and economic reforms necessary to make the blacks feel that they really were citizens of their own country.

So yes, 1948 was a turning-point; but not perhaps such a sharp one as seemed to be the case in 1948 and the years immediately following.

Unit 1 Review

The cover of the programme of the 1938 Blood River Centenary Celebrations. Two ox-wagons modelled on those used by the Voortrekkers and accompanied by people in trekker dress set out from Cape Town in August 1938 and arrived at the Voortrekker Monument site (see page 28) near Pretoria in December. In all the towns and villages they passed through, enthusiastic Afrikaner crowds gathered.

Questions

1 **a** Look at the picture above. Who were the Voortrekkers and what happened in 1838 which Afrikaners thought worthy of national remembrance?
b Why do you think that the artist made a point of showing ox-wagons?
c D. F. Malan and his Purified National Party strongly supported these centenary celebrations. Why do you think they did so?
d What would (i) most blacks and (ii) English-speaking whites have thought of the celebrations?

2 On page 6, the 1946 census divides the South African population into four racial groups.
a What were these groups?
b Explain how each had come to be in South Africa.
c Explain the main differences in their situations in 1948.

3 How did the discovery of gold and diamonds change:
a European interest in South Africa?
b patterns of black employment?

4 **a** What is meant by the term 'segregation'?
b In what ways was South Africa segregated in 1948?

5 **a** What was the result of the 1948 election?
b Was it really a turning point in South African history?

Part 2: The nature of the apartheid state
Unit 2 · Apartheid and black resistance, 1948–60

One of the largest crowds then seen in South Africa, mainly white Afrikaners, celebrate the opening of the Voortrekker Monument in 1949.

This huge granite building stands on a hill outside Pretoria. It was designed in honour of the Afrikaner nation, and both inside and outside shows Afrikaners triumphing over the British, and the whites over the blacks. Daniel Malan, the new Prime Minister, opened it.

In his victory speech after the 1948 general election, Malan had proclaimed: 'Today South Africa belongs to us once more!' By 'us', he meant Afrikaners. He and his ministers set to work to make sure that South Africa continued to belong to them. Their method was apartheid, which, as you have read, means 'separateness'.

Making the apartheid state, 1948–58

The aims of apartheid

The word 'apartheid' was first used in discussions about politics and race in the 1930s by Afrikaner thinkers who led the Afrikaner nationalist revival of those years.

Their main message was that the races in South Africa needed to be separated more, not less. For them, the history of South Africa proved that different races could not live together in peace. One race was bound to bully the others, and close contact between the races always caused fear and hatred. The only way forward for South Africa was for the different races to live apart and develop their lives separately. Though some blacks would need to work in white areas, this could only be on a temporary basis. Their permanent homes were in the reserves, the only places where they had political rights. They would never have political rights in 'white' areas since they would swamp the whites by sheer numbers.

Of course, South Africa was already a very segregated country. However, apartheid was to make segregation more far-reaching and harmful to the black majority. And it did so just when much of the rest of the world was moving strongly in the opposite direction.

The Tomlinson Report

In 1950, Prime Minister Malan appointed Professor Tomlinson to chair a commission to advise how apartheid should work in practice. He reported in 1955. Source 1 on the next page shows how he recommended the races should be separated.

Tomlinson advised the government that the separation of the races could work, as long as it was prepared to pay. It should divide the reserves up into seven areas, each the 'homeland' of a separate black people – for example, the Xhosa and the Zulu. Over the next ten years it should spend £104 million to improve farming in the homelands and set up factories on their borders. In due course, the homelands would provide enough employment for most blacks, and many blacks would move or be moved from 'white' towns and cities so that the whites would no longer be outnumbered there.

Defects of the Tomlinson proposals

This was very neat and comforting for the white population. However, the arithmetic did not add up. Though the area set aside for the black

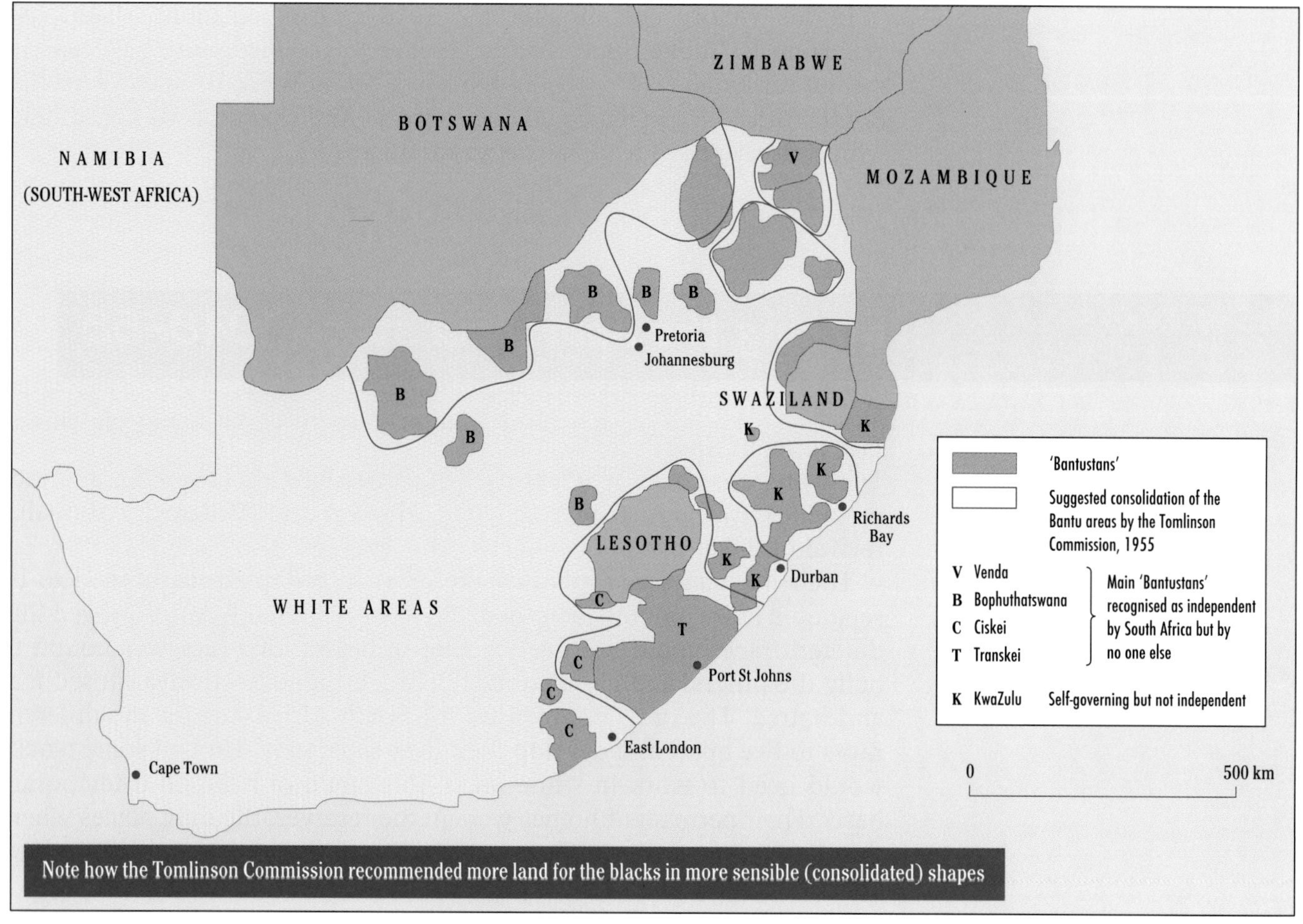

Source 1

The Tomlinson proposals (1955) and the actual 'Bantustans' of the 1970s and 1980s.

homelands was among the most fertile and well-watered parts of an otherwise dry country, it was still only 13 per cent of the whole of South Africa, far too little when the blacks made up nearly 70 per cent of the population.

Tomlinson made two other serious miscalculations. First, he predicted that black numbers would increase much more slowly than in fact they did (see pages 72–73). Second, he failed to realise how fast factories run by whites would expand and pull more and more black labour into the white towns.

To make matters worse, the government refused to spend anything like as much as Tomlinson advised either on farming improvements or on businesses in the reserves. The result was that many blacks lived in dreadful poverty in homelands not fertile enough to support such numbers. Many others sought to live in the cities where the jobs were, only to be harassed continually by the apartheid laws which aimed to keep them out.

The 'baaskap' apartheid laws

Despite these fundamental flaws in the Tomlinson Report, the Nationalists pressed ahead with a series of laws to put into effect the first phase of apartheid. This phase lasted until the late 1950s and is usually described as 'baaskap' or 'white supremacy'.

Source 2 shows some of the main laws which the National government passed between 1948 and 1956.

Source 2

The main apartheid laws, 1948–56.

The Prohibition of Mixed Marriages Act (1949) made it illegal for people of different races to marry.

The Population Registration Act (1950) forced each South African into a particular racial group, since how could the races be separated unless government officials knew who belonged to which race? The problem was that generations of mixed marriages made this almost impossible to do accurately. One aim of this law was to prevent the Cape Coloureds from being treated as whites. Coloured families suffered the most, with different members of the same family in some cases being classified differently!

The Group Areas Act (1950) gave the government the power to declare areas 'for whites only' and move blacks out, whether or not they wished to go.

The Suppression of Communism Act (1950) not only banned communism but also any political group 'which aimed to bring about political ... change by the promotion of disturbances and disorder'.

The Native Laws Amendment Act (1952) controlled the movement of blacks in and out of towns and cities.

The Abolition of Passes Act (1952) contradicted its title and tightened up the pre-war pass laws. It forced all black men living in 'white' areas to carry a pass or reference book containing personal details including their racial group. Without a pass, living and working in a 'white' area were illegal. Renewing a pass often involved waiting in queues for days outside government offices. This much-hated law was strictly enforced by police raids.

The Separate Amenities Act (1953) designated all public services and public spaces with signs specifying 'Europeans Only' and 'Non-Europeans Only' – for example, post offices, trains and buses, parks and beaches. Seldom were the non-European spaces anything like as pleasant as the European ones.

The Bantu Education Act (1953) brought black education fully under government control. Black schools had to provide different courses from white ones and teach in their ethnic language, not in English. Pupils should be prepared for life in the homelands, not the white cities. The government closed down many mission schools.

The Separate Representation of Voters Act (1956) ended the right of the Cape Coloureds to vote with the whites in elections. In future they could only vote for four white representatives in the House of Assembly.

Source 3

A cartoon by David Marais in the *Cape Times* in 1959: 'When I ask you for proof, I mean your identity card!'

Source 4

The Separate Amenities law in action. A 'Whites only' sign on the seashore.

Questions

Re-read pages 28–32.

1 What were the main aims of apartheid?

2 Study Source 1.
 a How did Tomlinson intend to reduce the number of blacks in white areas?
 b Suggest some of the other weaknesses of the proposals.

3 Study Source 2. List those apartheid laws which were aimed mainly at:
 a dividing up the different races;
 b controlling the movement of blacks.

4 Newspaper cartoons are intended to be amusing comments on events or issues in the news.
 a What issue is the cartoonist commenting on in Source 3?
 b Explain how likely you think black people were to be amused by the cartoon.

Peaceful opposition, 1948–60

How did blacks react to the 'apartheid' laws?

Terrible rioting in Natal in 1949 between Africans and Indians had led to more than 140 deaths and convinced the political leaders of the two groups that they must work together against their common enemy, the National government.

Simultaneously, the Youth Leaguers were growing impatient with Dr Xuma, who disliked mass action. They forced him to resign, and Dr Moroka succeeded him as President of the ANC. Walter Sisulu became Secretary-General, and Nelson Mandela and Oliver Tambo joined the national executive.

The Youth League leaders were now in control. They knew the Nationalists would take no notice of polite opposition, so they decided on a programme of action – strikes, demonstrations and non-cooperation with the government. A National Day of Protest in June 1950 was an early example of this more fiery resistance.

Source 1

An ANC poster of June 1950.

NATIONAL DAY OF PROTEST

MONDAY, 26TH JUNE, 1950

Begins the all out struggle for Freedom.

Dr. J. S. Moroka, President-General of the African National Congress, supported by Leaders of the South African Indian Congress, and African Peoples' Organisation calls upon all South Africans to REFRAIN FROM GOING TO WORK ON THIS DAY.

- DEFEAT THE SUPPRESSION OF COMMUNISM AND THE GROUP AREAS BILLS WHICH WILL TURN OUR COUNTRY INTO A POLICE STATE.
- DON'T ALLOW MALAN GOVERNMENT'S OPPRESSIVE FASCIST MEASURES TO CRUSH OUR LIVES & LIBERTIES!
- FIGHT FOR FREEDOM — PASS LAWS AND POLICE RAIDS MUST GO! LAND, VOTES AND DECENT WAGES FOR ALL!

'Tis better to sacrifice all in the struggle for Freedom rather than live as slaves.

African, Coloured, Indian and European Democrats—FREEDOM NOT SERFDOM!

The Defiance Campaign, 1952

The 300th anniversary of the arrival of Jan van Riebeeck at the Cape was on 26 June 1952 (see page 7). Since the government planned celebrations all over the country, the ANC decided to use the day to show the whites in South Africa and the whole world how wrong apartheid was and how black patience was running out.

The Defiance Campaign was planned as a peaceful black protest against the apartheid laws. Demonstrators invited arrest by ignoring 'Europeans Only' signs at post offices and railway stations. 'Hey, Malan', many of them would chant, 'open the jail doors, we want to enter, we volunteers!' More than 8,000 were arrested that summer during peaceful protests but, in October, riots took place in which both blacks and whites were killed. The government introduced new laws. Defiance could lead to a whipping as well as to fines and imprisonment. The protest leaders might be sent to jail for up to three years, rather than a month or two. By the end of 1952 the campaign had run out of steam, but the ANC's membership had risen from 7,000 to 100,000.

The Defiance Campaign gave confidence to the opponents of the government that further mass protest could bring political changes. They realised that, like other revolutionary movements, they needed a manifesto, a clear statement of the kind of South Africa they dreamed of creating. So they met together and drafted the Freedom Charter, the most important single document of the resistance to apartheid.

The Freedom Charter, 1955

In June 1955 the ANC and other opposition groups met at the village of Kliptown, near Johannesburg. They called themselves the Congress of the People. Watched by the police, their first act was to present prizes to three well-known anti-apartheid campaigners.

One was Father Trevor Huddleston, an English priest, who had done everything he could to prevent the government using the Group Areas Act to destroy his parish, the mainly black-owned township of Sophiatown. Another was Yusuf Dadoo, the Indian leader, and the third was Chief Albert Luthuli, who had recently succeeded Dr Moroka as President of the ANC. Only Huddleston could appear to receive his prize, since the other two were banned from taking part in political meetings.

Mandela and Sisulu were banned too, but they travelled out to Kliptown, staying on the edge of the crowd lest they were seen by the police and arrested. After the award of the prizes, the Freedom Charter was read out paragraph by paragraph and approved by the Congress.

The Charter, predicted the banned Chief Luthuli, 'would be a torchlight in whatever dark skies overcast the path to freedom'. For Mandela 'it captured the hopes and dreams of the people and acted as a blueprint for the liberation struggle and the future of the nation'. Source 2 gives an idea of why they considered it so vital for the future of South Africa.

Source 2

The main points of the Freedom Charter of 1955.

1 THE PEOPLE SHALL GOVERN
Every man and woman shall have the right to vote for and stand as a candidate for all bodies which make laws....

2 ALL NATIONAL GROUPS SHALL HAVE EQUAL RIGHTS
All apartheid laws shall be set aside.

3 ALL PEOPLE SHALL SHARE IN THE NATION'S WEALTH
The national wealth of our country, the heritage of all South Africans, shall be restored to the people; the mineral wealth beneath the soil, the banks and monopoly industries shall be transferred to the ownership of the people....

4 THE LAND SHALL BE SHARED BY THOSE WHO WORK IT!
Restriction of land ownership on a racial basis shall be ended, and all land re-divided among those who work it....

5 ALL SHALL BE EQUAL BEFORE THE LAW!
No-one shall be imprisoned, deported or restricted without fair trial.

6 ALL SHALL ENJOY HUMAN RIGHTS!
The law shall guarantee to all the right to speak, to organise, to meet together, to publish, to preach, to worship, and to educate their children.... Pass laws, permits and all other laws restricting these freedoms shall be abolished.

7 THERE SHALL BE WORK AND SECURITY!
All who work shall be free to form trade unions.... Men and women of all races shall receive equal pay for equal work ... sick leave for all workers and maternity leave on full pay for all working mothers....

8 THE DOORS OF LEARNING AND CULTURE SHALL BE OPENED!
Education shall be free, compulsory, universal and equal for all children....

9 THERE SHALL BE HOUSES, SECURITY AND COMFORT!
Rent and prices shall be lowered, food plentiful, and no-one shall go hungry; free medical care ... shall be provided ... slums demolished ... the aged, orphans, the disabled and sick cared for by the state....

10 LET THERE BE PEACE AND FRIENDSHIP!
Let all who love their people and their country now say, as we say here: THESE FREEDOMS WE SHALL FIGHT FOR, SIDE BY SIDE, THROUGHOUT OUR LIVES UNTIL WE HAVE WON OUR LIBERTY.

Source 3

The start of the Treason Trials. The 156 accused pose cheerfully for the camera.

The government counter-attacks: the Treason Trials

The government soon took counter-action. In 1956 it arrested and charged with high treason 156 people, including most of the leaders of the ANC and of the Indian community. Government lawyers tried to prove that the Freedom Charter was communist and that the accused were plotting violent revolution. They failed to make their case and all the accused were eventually released. However, they had been on trial and out of action for five years, so, during these years, the opposition was seriously weakened.

Questions

1 Study Source 2. If the South African government had agreed to points 4, 6 and 8 of the Charter, which of the apartheid laws on page 31 would it have had to abolish?

2 You are a senior white police officer at Kliptown and a supporter of the National Party. Write a report to the government about the Kliptown meeting which describes what happened and assesses how dangerous for the National government it could be.

Women's resistance

Women, black and white, played a very active and brave part in resisting apartheid. Who were they and what forms did their resistance take?

Why and how did women resist apartheid?

Apartheid placed heavy burdens on black women. In rural areas, the migrant system might take their husbands away for months on end and leave them to care for the animals and crops as well as the children. A major worry for urban women were the complicated 'Section 10 laws' which the government used to control black movement into cities. When strictly enforced they often broke up marriages if only one partner had residence rights.

Anti-pass law demonstrations

When, in 1955, the government announced that black women as well as men would have to carry passes, women and men joined together in large, peaceful demonstrations such as the one shown in Source 1. One of the leaders in Johannesburg was Albertina Sisulu, wife of Walter. She led the

Source 1

Women demonstrate against the hated pass laws, Johannesburg, 1955.

demonstration in Market Square which ended with passes being burnt. For this she was arrested and imprisoned. She refused to stop criticising the government and was in and out of jail or banned (which meant that she could not take part in any political activities nor lead a normal social life) for seventeen years. The mother of five children and a full-time nurse, in 1963 she was the first woman to be held in prison under the 90-day law which allowed the government to hold people in solitary confinement for up to 90 days without trial. At the same time Walter was in hiding and the government had arrested her eldest son, Max. A 14-year-old cousin had to look after the four younger children.

The Black Sash organisation

A group of white women founded this organisation in 1955 to fight the National Party's plans to end Coloured voting rights. Members held demonstrations wearing black sashes of mourning. Later they gave help to blacks living in cities – for example, by offering legal advice on Section 10.

Black and white women work together

In 1956 the Federation of South African Women (FSAW) – whose president was the black Lilian Ngoyi, an active trade unionist, and whose secretary was the white social worker Helen Joseph – led an enormous march on the Union Buildings in Pretoria, the heart of white power. Twenty thousand women came, each carrying a letter of protest against apartheid, especially the hated pass laws. Helen Joseph, a white social worker and Ngoyi's secretary, described the protest:

Source 2
From Helen Joseph's autobiography, *Side by Side*, 1986.

We took those letters of protest ... to the offices of the Prime Minister, Johannes Strijdom. He was not there. We flooded his office with them and returned to the thousands of women, waiting for us packed tightly together.... Lilian Ngoyi called on them to stand in silent protest. As she raised her right arm in the Congress salute, 20,000 arms went up and stayed there for those endless minutes. We knew that all over South Africa, women in the cities and towns were gathered together in protest. We were not just 20,000, but many thousand more....

At the end of that half-hour, Lilian began to sing, softly at first 'Nkosi Sikelele' (Lord, give strength to Africa!). For the blacks it has become their national anthem and the voices rose, joining Lilian, ever louder and stronger. Then I heard a new song, composed specially for the protest, 'Wathint' a bafazi, wa uthint' imbolodo uzo kufa' (You have struck a rock, you have tampered with the women, you shall be destroyed). It was meant for Strijdom.

Winnie Mandela

Nelson Mandela's second wife, Winnie, kept the flag of resistance flying in the 1970s and 1980s. A brave and fiery woman, she gained much popularity among the young people of Soweto where she lived. Frequently detained or imprisoned, the government eventually moved her and her daughters to the small town of Brandfort in the Orange Free State. This cruel act increased her international fame. Her later years were clouded by violence, scandal and the break up of her marriage.

Source 3 Helen Joseph and Lilian Ngoyi reunited after ten years of banning.

White female opponents of apartheid

Of the white critics of the government, some of the fiercest were white women. In the 1940s Margaret Ballinger was one of the white native representatives in the Assembly and never rested in her defence of black interests. Nor did Helen Suzman, for many years in the 1960s and 1970s the only Progressive Party MP in the all-white Parliament.

Ruth First, journalist and member both of the ANC and the Communist Party, was another early victim of the infamous 90-day law. She was arrested in 1963, in connection with the Rivonia plot (see page 47), held for ninety days in solitary confinement, released and immediately arrested again, even though she was the mother of three children. Finally, after 117 days, she was freed without being charged. She later left South Africa and worked at the Centre of African Studies at Maputo University in Mozambique. There the South African secret service murdered her with a letter bomb.

Questions

Re-read pages 36–38

1 Source 1 shows women demonstrating against the pass laws.

a Look back to Source 3 on page 14 and explain what the pass laws were.

b Why do you think these women felt that the pass laws were against freedom and justice?

c This was a peaceful demonstration, yet Albertina Sisulu was imprisoned for helping to lead it. Why do you think the police treated the demonstrators so harshly?

2 Lilian Ngoyi and Helen Joseph (Source 3) were banned as a result of their political activities (see Source 2). This meant that they were not allowed to take part in political activities and were forbidden to see each other. Which aspects of their protest do you think made the government treat them so harshly?

Unit 2 Review

Cartoon by David Marais from the *Cape Times* of 1957: 'You haven't had 15 years' continuous residence or ten years' continuous employment. You are not qualified to live anywhere at all!'

Questions

1 The man with the paper in his hand is Dr Hendrik Verwoerd, Minister for Native Affairs.

a What apartheid regulation does the cartoon caption suggest Verwoerd is holding?

b What was the aim of this regulation?

c Why was it so hated by the blacks?

d What does the cartoon suggest about the attitude towards the National government of the *Cape Times* newspaper?

2 How did apartheid change life for:

a rural blacks;

b urban blacks;

c urban whites?

3 **a** What were the Programme of Action; the Defiance Campaign; the Congress of the People; the FSAW March in Pretoria; the Treason Trials?

b How successful were the ANC and the other opposition groups between 1948 and 1960?

4 When Dr Verwoerd resigned as Minister of Native Affairs in 1958, Afrikaner politicians and newspapers showered him with praise. 'It is he who systematically put into effect the policy of separate development,' wrote *Die Transvaler*. 'Previously there was chaos, now order,' said his successor, M. C. de Wet Nel. How might Nel have described this new system and order in more detail to the white Parliament?

Unit 3 · Verwoerd's apartheid, 1958–74

Verwoerd and the Bantustans

Of all the National Party leaders, Hendrik Verwoerd was the most powerful and confident. He masterminded a second phase of apartheid. His aim was to make apartheid internationally respectable by allowing blacks to develop separately in 'homelands' which could become independent nations, or 'Bantustans'.

Verwoerd was born in the Netherlands in 1901. His parents emigrated to South Africa when he was two, his father wanting to be a missionary.

The young Verwoerd did outstandingly well at school and at Stellenbosch University, near Cape Town, where he studied theology and was given his first job as a lecturer in psychology. He was already an enthusiastic nationalist with a lively interest in politics. He joined the Broederbond in the 1930s and in 1937 became editor of a major Afrikaner newspaper, *Die Transvaler*. He gave Daniel Malan his warm support and was a bitter critic of Jan Smuts.

Source 1

Verwoerd (left) arriving in London for the 1961 Commonwealth Conference which led to South Africa being driven out of the Commonwealth. He is being welcomed by Duncan Sandys, the British Colonial Secretary.

Malan rewarded him in 1950 with the key post of Minister for Native Affairs. When Strijdom, Malan's successor as Prime Minister, died in 1958, Verwoerd was his obvious successor. He dominated his party until 1966, when he was stabbed to death, sitting in his usual place in the Parliament at Cape Town, by a deranged official.

Verwoerd was unusually intelligent, hard-working and determined. Such personal qualities in a leader would, in many situations, have brought great benefits to a country. However, since in Verwoerd's case they were linked to an impossible plan for South Africa's future, they were seriously harmful. As far as the blacks were concerned, he was an evil tyrant. Chief Luthuli put it like this:

Source 2

Albert Luthuli, *Let My People Go*, 1963.

If any man is remembered as the author of our calamity, it will be he.

The idea of separate development

Verwoerd believed that he had a God-given mission to secure the future of Christian white South Africa. He realised that in a changing world where many black African colonies were winning independence and where international opinion would no longer tolerate old-style white supremacy, the image of apartheid needed to be changed. His solution was to offer to the blacks the apparent chance to develop as they wanted, separately from the whites in their homelands, which, if their inhabitants wished, could become completely independent nations. These he called Bantu National Units, although his critics preferred the term 'Bantustans'. In a message to the people of South Africa he said:

Source 3

Hendrik Verwoerd, message to the people of South Africa, 1958.

I am seeking justice for all groups.... The policy of separate development is designed for the happiness, security and stability provided by their home language and administration for the Bantu as well as the whites.

The Bantustans

By the Promotion of the Bantu Self-Government Act of 1959 he created eight Bantu National Units based on a division of the reserves along tribal lines (see Source 1 on page 30). He encouraged chiefs to be active politically and to look forward to greater independence. The Transkei became self-governing in 1963 and 'independent' in 1976 (see Source 4). Mantanzima, its first Prime Minister, was the chiefs' choice, not the people's. Other Bantustans to move to 'independence' were Bophuthatswana, Venda and the Ciskei.

No other nations recognised the Bantustans as independent states and it is easy to understand why, simply by looking at the map. They were far too small – geographical fragments with little economic or social strength.

Source 4

An independent Bantustan: Chief Sigcau of the Transkei arrives at Parliament to be sworn in as president, 25 October 1976.

Most importantly, they did not have any real support from the local black people who saw them for what they were: artificial creations of an essentially hostile white government.

Chief Luthuli, President of the ANC, made clear the attitude of most black leaders to the Bantustan policy in his autobiography, *Let My People Go*.

Source 5

Albert Luthuli, *Let My People Go*, 1963.

Inside this closed world [of the Bantustans] there is no hint, not the remotest suggestion of democratic rule.... The modes* of government ... are neither democratic nor African. The Act makes our chiefs, quite straightforwardly and simply, into minor puppets and agents of the Big Dictator*.

* **modes** Methods
* **the Big Dictator** The white Minister of Bantu Administration and Development.

Weaknesses of Verwoerd's policy

Like Tomlinson before him, Verwoerd looked forward to the time when, because of developments in the Bantustans, blacks would move to them from the cities and the proportion of whites to blacks in the 'white' areas would shift to the whites' advantage. He was confident that by 1978 this shift would be clearly visible.

Verwoerd refused to face the realities of South Africa's economic and population growth. The country's growing manufacturing industries needed a well-educated and well-trained black workforce living close to their factories. They also wanted a better-off urban black population to buy their products. And since the black population was growing so fast (from 11 million in 1960 to 21 million in 1980), his hope for 'whiter' cities was a fantasy. But when people told him that his policies did not meet the country's economic needs, he had a short answer:

Source 6

Hendrik Verwoerd, quoted by A. Sparks, *The Mind of South Africa*, 1990.

If South Africa has to choose between being poor and white or rich and multi-racial, then it must rather choose to be white.

In fact, Verwoerd's policies were astonishingly blinkered. He did not seriously consider increasing the amount of lands the Bantustans should have, despite the obvious unfairness of just 13 per cent of the land for 70 per cent of the population. Nor would he allow white businesses to provide employment within the Bantustans, though his officials had more than enough evidence of overcrowding in the reserves, .

Moreover, much of him remained at heart an unashamed white supremacist. It was he who as Minister for Native Affairs had taken the Bantu Education Act through Parliament in 1953. He declared that:

Source 7

Hendrik Verwoerd, speaking in the South African Senate, 1953.

The Natives will be taught from childhood to realise that equality with Europeans is not for them.... What is the use of teaching the Bantu mathematics when he cannot use it in practice.... There is no place for the Bantu child above the level of certain forms of labour.

White support for Verwoerd

For the whites, however, Verwoerd seemed just what they needed. When the rest of the world was attacking them for the wickedness of their race policies, he refused to apologise. On the contrary, his answer was to explain how 'separate development' should be as good for the blacks as for the whites. That it could never work and was bound to lead to black suffering on a colossal scale occurred to few of them. One of the most remarkable things about apartheid was its ability to keep black hardship out of sight of the whites, because it shifted the races apart wherever possible. In Johannesburg, most whites lived in the northern suburbs, fifteen kilometres or more from Soweto, its main black township. In Cape Town the attractive white suburbs kept close to the slopes of Table Mountain, while the black and Coloured townships were scattered distantly across the sandy, windswept Cape Flats.

The whites rewarded Verwoerd and his National Party with their votes, as Source 8 shows.

Source 8

White general election results, 1948–66.

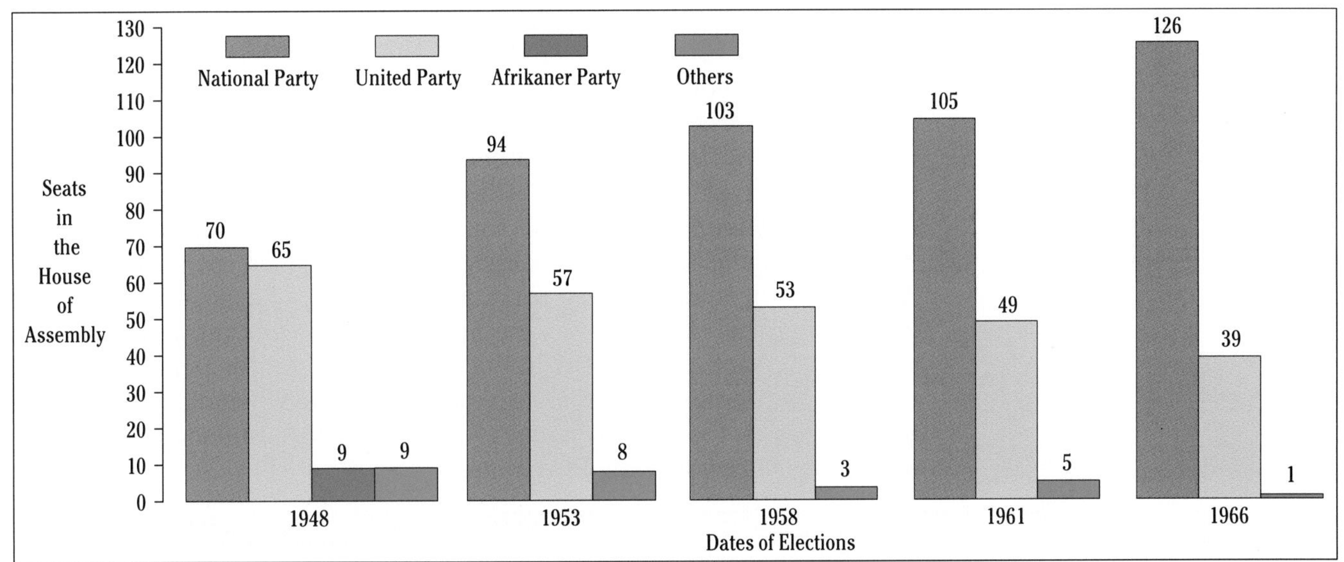

Questions

1 Study pages 40–43 and Source 3.
a What did Verwoerd mean by 'separate development'?
b How did he aim to get 'justice for all groups'?

2 Study page 41 and Source 4.
a What was the Transkei?
b What is happening in the photograph?

3 Study Sources 2 and 5.
a Who was Chief Luthuli?
b How seriously would you take his comments on Verwoerd's policies?
c What were his main criticisms?

4 Look back to pages 30–31.
a What did 'baaskap' mean?
b How did Malan's 'baaskap' apartheid laws differ from Verwoerd's apartheid policies?

Sharpeville and the 'Spear of the People', 1960–64

A new black group, the Pan-African Congress (PAC), began more anti-pass law demonstrations in 1960. At Sharpeville the police shot and killed sixty-nine demonstrators. Both the ANC and PAC decided that further peaceful protest was pointless and formed underground terrorist sections.

Black resistance and violence

Sharpeville and Langa, March 1960

In 1959, the PAC, led by Robert Sobukwe, had split away from the ANC which seemed to it too cautious, too multi-racial and too influenced by Communists. In 1960 both organisations planned massive, peaceful anti-pass law demonstrations, the PAC making clear that they hoped that many of them would be arrested.

Early on the morning of Monday, 21 March, Sobukwe began the campaign in the Transvaal by marching with some of his supporters to the police station of Orlando township. They were immediately arrested. Fifty-six kilometres away to the south-west in the Sharpeville township near Vereeniging, a large and noisy crowd surrounded the police station. A young policeman lost his nerve and fired into the crowd, as did his colleagues. They killed sixty-nine and wounded another 180, many by shots in the back. Meanwhile in the Cape, at Langa township, the police ordered the demonstrators to leave and then baton-charged them. The demonstrators then threw stones. The police responded with bullets, killing two and wounding forty-nine.

Source 1

Sharpeville after the shootings on 21 March 1960.

Consequences of the shootings

Sharpeville and Langa shocked international opinion. From all over the world came demands that apartheid should end. As white businessmen asked themselves whether the country had a peaceful future there was a serious financial crisis. Trouble continued in the Cape. On 30 March, Philip Kgosana, the local PAC leader, led 30,000 marchers right into the centre of the city and to the Houses of Parliament to protest against police violence. Cape Town had never seen anything like it. The local police chief promised Kgosana that, if he got the demonstrators home peacefully, he could have the meeting he wanted with the Minister of Justice the next day. Kgosana carried out his part of the bargain; the police did not, arresting him when he turned up as arranged for the interview.

After some dithering, the government decided on total repression. It declared a state of emergency, called out its reserve army, arrested thousands of the leading demonstrators and outlawed the ANC and PAC. Demonstrations and rioting came to an end.

The end of moderate protest

The message of Sharpeville, Langa and government repression to most black leaders was that the time for peaceful protest had passed. As Luthuli put it:

Source 2

Albert Luthuli, from a speech in 1961, accepting the Nobel Peace Prize.

> Who will deny that thirty years of my life have been spent knocking in vain, patiently, moderately and modestly at a closed and barred door. What have been the fruits of moderation? The past thirty years have seen the greatest number of laws restricting our rights and progress, until today we have reached a stage where we have almost no rights at all.

Mandela used the African saying, 'Sebatana ha se bokwe ka diatla' (the attacks of the wild beast cannot be fought off with only bare hands), to persuade the ANC leaders that they must now turn to violence. He went underground to form 'Umkhonto we Sizwe' (the Spear of the People), usually known as MK, and to plan a campaign of sabotage. Oliver Tambo had already gone overseas to re-establish the ANC, banned in South Africa, in exile. Similarly, the PAC set up its terrorist arm, Poqo (we go it alone) and its organisation-in-exile. Sobukwe was already in prison and would remain there for another nine years.

Source 3

MK in action: electricity power lines blown up in 1961.

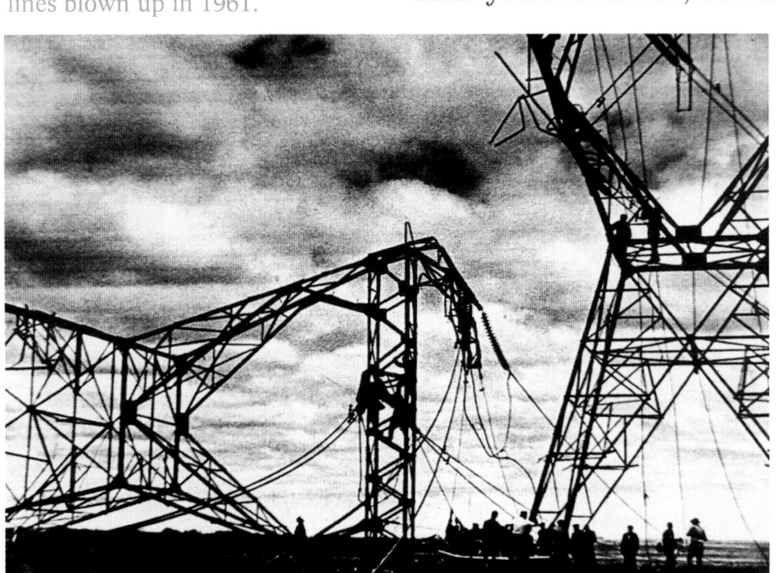

Mandela and the Spear of the People (MK)

MK concentrated on sabotage and aimed to avoid loss of life. It launched its first attacks in 1961, its chief targets being power stations (see Source 3) and government offices. Simultaneously it published a leaflet, explaining its actions.

Source 4

Nelson Mandela, *Long Walk to Freedom*, 1994.

> The time comes in the life of any nation when there remain only two choices: submit or fight. That time has come to South Africa. We shall not submit and we have no choice but to hit back by all means within our power in defence of our people, our future and our freedom....

Mandela survived 'underground' for seventeen months, during which he travelled all over South Africa, trained as a guerrilla fighter in Ethiopia and visited Britain and many African states in search of advice and support. He became famous for his successes in staying a step ahead of the police and kept the newspapers informed about MK's plans by contacting them from public telephones. His most frequent disguises were as a chauffeur or garden boy and he had some narrow escapes. Once he found himself at a red traffic light next to the Chief of the Rand Security Police. Another time, standing at a street corner waiting to be collected by a friend, a black policeman clearly recognised him but simply gave him the ANC thumbs-up greeting and walked by.

His luck ran out in 1962 when he was caught in a police trap between Johannesburg and Durban, where he had been visiting Luthuli. His link with MK was not yet known so he was charged with 'leaving the country without permission' and given a five-year prison sentence.

The Rivonia Trial

The supposedly secret headquarters of MK was Lilliesleaf Farm in Rivonia on the edge of Johannesburg. Somehow the security police found out about it, perhaps through treachery, perhaps from careless talk.

Source 5

The end of the Rivonia Trial reported in the *Cape Argus*, 12 June 1964.

The Cape Argus

CITY LATE

EIGHT GUILTY IN RIVONIA TRIAL

Seven on all four charges and one on one count

BERNSTEIN FREED, REARRESTED

The Argus Correspondent

PRETORIA, Thursday.

SEVEN of the nine accused in the Rivonia sabotage trial were found guilty on all four counts in the Supreme Court, Pretoria, to-day.

The Judge President of the Transvaal (Mr. Justice Quartus de Wet) found that one accused, Ahmed Mohammat Kathrada, a Johannesburg Indian, was guilty on count two.

He found that Lionel Gabriel Bernstein, a Johannesburg architect, was not guilty and he was discharged. Before Bernstein could leave the court he was rearrested to the anguished cry of his wife, Hilda.

Col. Fred van Niekerk of the Security Police said that Bernstein had been arrested on a warrant.

Those found guilty on all four counts are: Nelson Rolihlahla Mandela, a Johannesburg attorney; Walter Max Ulitot Sisulu of Johannesburg; Dennis Theodore Goldberg, a civil engineer of Claremont, Cape Town; Govan Archibald Mbeki, a Port Elizabeth journalist; and Raymond Mhlaba (the State alleged that these five were members of the national high command); Elias Motsoaledi and Andrew Mlangeni.

The proceedings to-day lasted only three minutes. The court was packed from the time the doors were opened an hour and a half before the judge took the bench.

BERNSTEIN IN RAND COURT TO-MORROW

The Argus Correspondent

ACTION THREAT AGAINST DRIVER

MR. JUSTICE Q. DE WET, the Transvaal Judge President.

MRS. WINNIE MANDELA, wife of Nelson Mandela, leads her mother-in-law out of the crush after the verdict as the crowd shouts slogans and marches up and down.

MRS. BERNSTEIN AND DAUGHTER IN TEARS

When they raided the farm in 1963, not only did they arrest nine leading members of MK but they also discovered many papers outlining MK plans and linking Mandela to them.

The Rivonia Trial lasted from December 1963 to June 1964. The main charge – 'recruiting people for training in sabotage and guerrilla warfare for the purpose of violent revolution' – was extremely serious, and the prosecution demanded that the accused should be hanged. Mandela, Sisulu and six others were found guilty and sentenced not to death but to life imprisonment. The immense amount of international attention which the trial had aroused may have been a reason why the judge did not insist on the death penalty.

By the Rivonia arrests, the security police broke MK and the ANC inside South Africa. They were equally successful in breaking Poqo. None the less, the trial gave the accused the chance to tell South Africa and the world through the court why they had acted as they had. Mandela took immense trouble over his statement, which was a four-hour analysis of why the ANC had had to turn to violence. Here are some extracts:

Source 6

Nelson Mandela, commenting in the Rivonia Trial on government claims that he was a Communist and the ANC a communist organisation.

* **advocated** Argued in favour of.

I am not a Communist and have never been a member of the Communist Party....

The most important political document ever adopted by the ANC is the Freedom Charter. It is by no means the blueprint for a socialist state.... The ANC has never ... advocated* a revolutionary change in the economic structure of the country, nor ... ever condemned capitalist society....

It is true that there has often been close cooperation between the ANC and the Communist Party. But cooperation is merely proof of a common goal ... not of a complete community of interests.

Source 7

The final part of Mandela's statement. His lawyers strongly advised him to leave it out for fear it would encourage the judge to sentence him to death.

* **endorsed** Forced, compelled.

Africans want to be paid a living wage. Africans want to perform work which they are capable of doing, and not work which the government declares them to be capable of. Africans want to live where they can obtain work, and not to be endorsed* out of an area because they were not born there. Africans want to own land in places where they work ... and not be obliged to live in rented houses which they can never call their own ....

African men want to have their wives and children to live with them where they work, and not be forced into an unnatural existence in men's hostels. African women want to be with their menfolk and not be left permanently widowed in the reserves.... We want to travel in our own country and to seek work where we want to and not where the Labour Bureau tells us to. We want a just share in the whole of South Africa. We want security and a stake in society.

Above all, we want equal political rights, because without them our disabilities will be permanent. I know this sounds revolutionary to the whites of this country, because the majority of voters will be Africans. This makes the white man fear democracy. But this fear cannot be allowed to stand in the way of the only solution which will guarantee racial harmony and freedom for all. It is not true that the

* **the enfranchisement of all** Giving the right to vote to everybody.

enfranchisement of all* will result in racial domination. Political division, based on colour, is entirely artificial, and when it disappears, so will the domination of one colour group by another. The ANC has spent half a century fighting against racialism. When it triumphs, it will not change that policy....

This then is what the ANC is fighting for. Their struggle is a truly national one. It is a struggle of the African people, inspired by their own suffering and their own experience. It is a struggle for the right to live.

During my lifetime I have dedicated my life to this struggle of the African people. I have fought against white domination, and I have fought against black domination. I have cherished the idea of a democratic and free society in which all persons live together in harmony, and with equal opportunities. It is an ideal which I hope to live for and to achieve. But, if needs be, it is an ideal for which I am prepared to die.

Source 8

The British cartoonist Illingworth comments on the Mandela sentence.

Questions

1 Study pages 44–46 and Sources 1–4.
  a What happened in Sharpeville and Cape Town in March 1960?
  b What actions did the South African government take following these events?
  c How does this help to explain why most black leaders decided that there was no point in continuing peaceful protests?

2 Study pages 46–47 and Sources 4 and 5.
  a What happened at Rivonia in 1963?
  b Why was it such a setback to black resistance?

3 Study Sources 6 and 7.
  a What was Mandela's attitude towards (i) communism, (ii) the Freedom Charter, (iii) multi-racialism?
  b What kind of South Africa did Mandela look forward to?

4 What was the message to the British public of the cartoon in Source 8?

The human costs of apartheid

The National government intended its apartheid laws to change the way South Africans lived by separating the non-white groups from the whites wherever possible. This often meant changing the lives of the black and Coloured individuals whether they liked it or not. Sources 1–6 on the following pages have been chosen to illustrate some of those changes.

How were people's lives changed by apartheid?

Source 1 illustrates how one family was affected by the Population Registration Act of 1950 (see page 31). They were the Du Proft family, living in Cape Town:

Source 1

This account comes from research done by David Harrison for a BBC Television documentary about the Afrikaners, *The White Tribe of Africa*, 1981.

In 1950, just after the government introduced ... its new rules ... Raymond du Proft was serving in the police force.... He (a white) was twenty when he met a waitress named Diane Bassick.... They fell in love, but since she was classified Coloured ... they could only meet in secret.

Du Proft remembered how scared they were that they would be found out ... but before long they took a chance and started to live together. When their first son was born they found a house in an Afrikaans-speaking district and passed themselves off without difficulty as a white married couple. Eventually they had five children, all of whom were classified Coloured.... Regularly they applied for Diane and the children to be reclassified and just as regularly they were refused. So marriage remained out of the question. When their eldest boy, Graham, was nineteen, he started going out with an Afrikaans girl and she became pregnant. But again because he was classified Coloured and she was white they could not marry. Graham's response, in a moment of despair, was to throw himself under a train. He died instantly.

Source 2

The Du Proft parents with a photo of their son.

Source 3 illustrates the methods used to enforce the pass laws. Mark Mathabane remembers a police raid on his home in Alexandra township, Johannesburg, in 1965. The police smashed the door down, and though Mark's mother hid successfully in a wardrobe, they soon found his father.

Source 3

Mark Mathabane, *Kaffir Boy*, 1986.

My father ... was standing naked, his head bowed, in the middle of the bedroom.... In front of the bed was an old, brown table, against which my father's interrogator leaned, as he flashed his light all over my father, keeping him blinking all the time....

'Come, let's see your pass.' My father reached for his tattered overalls at the foot of the bed and from the back pocket he removed a small, square, bulky black book and handed it over to the policeman, who hurriedly flipped through it. Stonily, running his eyes up and down my father, he said, 'The bloody thing is not in order, you know?... Why isn't it in order? Mine is. Anyway, look here, as an old man you ought to be back in the Bantustan. My father is back there and living in peace....'

The policeman confirmed my suspicion of being fresh from the reserves. The authorities preferred his kind as policemen because of their ferociousness and blind obedience to white authority. They harboured a twisted fear and hatred of urban blacks.

'I'm working, nkosi*,' my father said. 'There are no jobs in the Bantustan....'

[Mark's father was arrested.] I stepped outside in time to see the two policemen, flanking my father, go up a rocky slope leading out of the yard. I saw more black policemen leading black men and women out of shacks.... Several children two or three years old, stood in tears outside smashed doors, imploring their mothers and fathers to come back.... Several red-necked white men in safari suits and fatigues, guns drawn, paced briskly about the entrance gates, shouting orders and supervising the round up....

My father spent two months doing hard labour on a white man's potato farm for his pass crimes.

* **nkosi** Sir.

Source 4

'Is your pass in order?' A typical, frequent and frightening meeting with the police in South Africa, 1950s.

Source 5

A child plays in the wasteland that was District 6, in Cape Town.

The Nationalists used the Group Areas Act to destroy black and Coloured communities, however deeply rooted, if they stood in areas which the government decided should be for whites only. Sophiatown near Johannesburg was destroyed in 1955; District 6, an area close to the centre of Cape Town with a population of 60,000, where Coloured people had lived since 1838, was destroyed in the 1970s. Source 5 shows the remains of that area.

One reason why the Nationalists were able to stay in power so long was that they created a strong security police force and allowed it to treat its opponents very harshly. Source 6 describes some of the methods it used.

Source 6

Roger Omond, *The Apartheid Handbook*, 1985.

Bannings

A banning order, signed by the Minister of Justice, prevented the named person from attending meetings, writing, broadcasting or being quoted, or leaving a particular district without permission from a magistrate. Any gathering which, in the opinion of the Minister of Justice, might 'seriously endanger the public peace' could also be banned. Political organisations like the ANC and PAC were banned....

Detention without trial

This was first used on a large scale during the Sharpeville crisis of 1960, when 11,700 people were detained under the state of emergency. People suspected of 'terrorism' could be held for up to thirty days in the first instance, and for longer if the Minister of Justice gave his approval. Detention without trial gave to the police plenty of opportunity for brutality and torture.

Between 1963 and 1985 at least 69 people died in police detention. Causes of death given include: 'suicide', 'falling out of a tenth floor window', 'slipped in the showers', 'fell down the stairs'.

Dr Neil Aggett died in detention in 1982 after being severely assaulted and not allowed to sleep.

Murder

A number of opponents of the government died in unexplained circumstances. That they were murdered by the security police is very probable, for example: Griffiths Mxenge stabbed to death in 1981, his wife Victoria shot and hacked to death in 1985; Abraham Tiro blown up by a parcel bomb in Botswana in the 1970s; Joe Gqabi shot in Zimbabwe in 1981.

Press censorship and harassment

Newspapers could not quote banned persons, and those critical of the government found themselves in difficulties. In 1967 the government successfully prosecuted Laurence Gandar, of the *Rand Daily Mail*, for publishing critical articles about prison conditions and in 1977 banned the *World*, a leading black newspaper.

Questions

1. Re-read pages 49–52.
   a Study Sources 1 and 2. Which aspects of this family's life were affected by the Population Registration Act?

   b How might their lives have been different if there had been no Act?
2. Sources 3 and 4 are about enforcing the pass laws. How did this change the lives of the people described in Source 3?
3. What changes did the Group Areas Act make to the people who had lived in areas like District 6 (Source 5)?
4. In Source 6, how might a person's life have been changed by:
   a a banning order;
   b detention without trial?
5. Incidents such as those described in Sources 1–6 made the South African government even more unpopular internationally. Why then do you think the government allowed such things to continue?

Unit 3 Review

After Sharpeville the opponents of apartheid turned to violence. Was this the right decision?

In June 1961, the ANC leaders met secretly to discuss whether they should give up non-violence, a central principle of their movement since its foundation. The government was taking ever tougher measures against its opponents. Peaceful protests were having no effect. A general strike organised a few days before had not been a success and there were already outbreaks of unplanned violence in some parts of the country.

The ANC leaders argued through the night. Some of them felt that violent methods were not only wrong but would lead to the destruction of the whole liberation movement. Others still believed that non-violent methods could work. Mandela, however, thought otherwise. He had three main arguments. First, the government had already turned to violence and took no notice of non-violence. Second, blacks were already turning to violence so the ANC needed to take the lead to make sure that whatever violence proved necessary would be well-planned and effective. Third, a sabotage campaign directed against buildings rather than people, though violent, would physically harm few people yet bring the government to its senses.

Mandela succeeded in carrying the leadership with him and MK was formed (see page 45).

Edward Feit, an American historian, argued in 1971 in his book *Urban Revolt in South Africa* that this decision was mistaken because violence frightened off popular support.

> The people, like the jungle, are neutral (neither on one side or the other). They will side with whoever protects them. Disorder makes life difficult.

Feit also argued that people, black as well as white, were suspicious of MK because it appeared to be communist controlled.

Questions

1 List the choices which faced the ANC in the summer of 1961.

2 How would you have argued if you had been at that crucial ANC meeting?

3 Outline the actions of MK between 1961 and 1963. Comment on the view that events proved Feit to be correct and Mandela wrong.

Part 3: The white minority in control

Unit 4 · White South Africa against the world, 1960–74

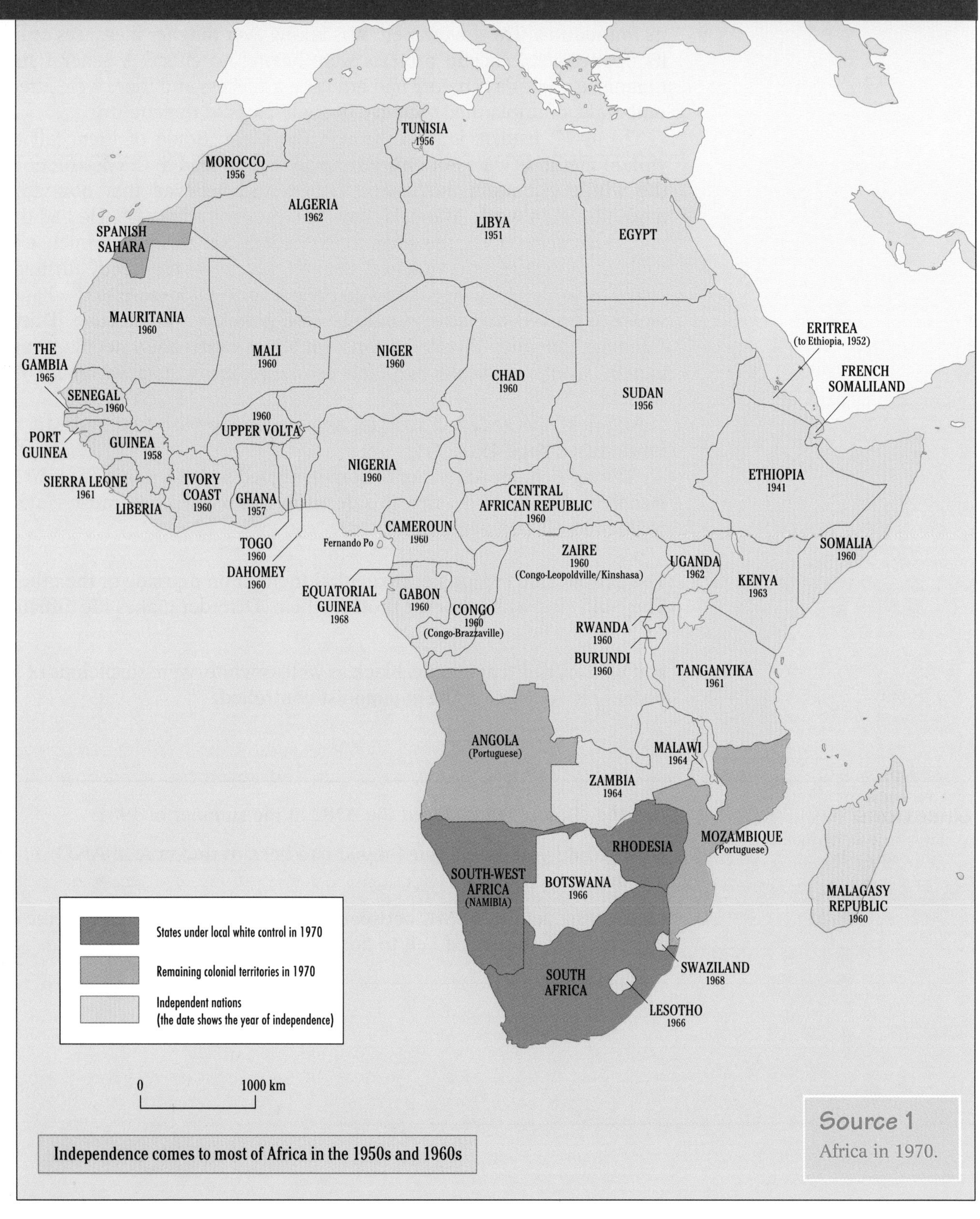

Source 1
Africa in 1970.

Changing Africa

In a rapidly changing world where many Asian and African nations were gaining their independence and racist attitudes were less tolerated, South Africa became one of its most unpopular countries. Many international organisations, notably the United Nations (UN) and the Organisation of African Unity (OAU), demanded that South Africa change its policies.

Why did world opinion turn against white South Africa?

The successes of African nationalism, 1956–68

While in South Africa a white Afrikaner government was smashing black nationalist opposition, elsewhere in Africa black nationalist movements were taking over from the white colonial powers, sometimes peacefully, sometimes by violence. The change began in the 1950s and, by 1968, only the Portuguese among the European colonial powers still clung on to their colonies. Virtually all of the rest of Africa, except the south, had black governments.

Macmillan's 'wind of change' speech, 1960

In February 1960, just a few weeks before the Sharpeville massacre, the British Prime Minister, Harold Macmillan, ended a tour of Africa in Cape Town. There he spoke to the white Parliament. He described his visits to other parts of Africa and explained how strong African nationalism had become. He commented:

Source 2

Harold Macmillan, speech to the South African Parliament, February 1960.

> The wind of change is blowing throughout the continent .... Whether we like it or not, this growth of national consciousness is a political fact ....
>
> The aim [of our modern Commonwealth*] ... is to create a society which respects the rights of individuals ... in which individual merit and merit alone is the criterion for a man's advancement, whether political or economic ....

* **Commonwealth** An association of nations consisting of Britain and the states that were once colonies in the British Empire.

Macmillan made it clear that Britain and the Commonwealth found South Africa's apartheid policies unacceptable. Verwoerd answered at once on behalf of white South Africa, saying:

Source 3

Hendrik Verwoerd, speech to the South African Parliament, February, 1960.

> There must not only be justice to the black man in Africa but also to the white man.... This is our only motherland. We have nowhere else to go.

South Africa and the British Commonwealth

Verwoerd then decided to try to achieve the dream of many Afrikaner Nationalists, to make South Africa a republic with its own president instead of the British monarch as head of state. An all-white referendum in 1960 agreed with him by a small but clear majority and, in 1961, South

Source 4

A pitch invasion during the Springbok (South African) Rugby tour of Britain in 1969. Demonstrations like this eventually led to a virtually complete ban on overseas sporting tours, which upset sports-mad white South Africans greatly.

Africa became a republic. Verwoerd had hoped to stay a member of the Commonwealth, but at a Commonwealth Conference in London he had to face such criticisms of apartheid that he took his country out.

Anti-apartheid movements

Worldwide disgust about apartheid increasingly isolated South Africa during the 1960s. All over the world, anti-apartheid groups were set up which organised demonstrations and trade and sporting boycotts (see Sources 4 and 5). Verwoerd, and Vorster, his successor, helped to provoke the sporting boycotts. In 1966 Verwoerd refused entry to some Maoris whom the New Zealand Rugby authorities had selected to tour South Africa. Two years later, Vorster did the same to Basil D'Oliveira, a Cape Coloured cricketer who had made his career in Britain so successfully that he was selected by England for a South African tour.

Source 5

Anti-apartheid demonstrators, London, 1976.

The United Nations and the Organisation of African Unity (OAU)

Every new black African nation naturally wanted the end of apartheid so, as each joined the UN, that international organisation became increasingly critical of South Africa. In 1963, the black African nations came together to form the OAU which, at its first meeting, made the abolition of apartheid in South Africa one of its main aims. In 1969, in Lusaka, the capital of Zambia, the leaders of fourteen eastern and central African nations issued the Lusaka Manifesto, making clear their readiness to help the blacks of South Africa in their struggle against white rule. Source 6 is a summary of its main points.

Source 6

The Lusaka Manifesto, 1969.

Point 6: In ... South Africa, there is an open and continued denial of the principles of human equality.... The societies of these territories are being deliberately organised so as to try and destroy these principles.

Point 8: Our stand towards southern Africa ... involves a rejection of racialism, not a reversal of existing racial domination. We believe that all the peoples who have made their homes in the countries of southern Africa are Africans, regardless of the colour of their skins.

Point 12: On the objective of liberation, we can neither surrender nor compromise. We have always preferred, and still prefer, to achieve it without physical violence.... But while peaceful progress is blocked by the actions of those at present in power in the states of southern Africa, we have no choice but to give to the peoples of those territories all the support of which we are capable in their struggle against their oppressors.

Vorster, who had by then succeeded Verwoerd as Prime Minister, replied:

Source 7

B. Vorster, speech to the South African Parliament, 1969.

* **not expendable** Cannot be got rid of.

The outside world and especially the war-mongering leaders on the African continent must understand very thoroughly that the white man in South Africa is not expendable .... Let them spit as much fire as they want to about the so-called immorality of apartheid ... we in South Africa know that it is the only feasible policy....

Questions

1 Re-read pages 54–57.
a What was the OAU?
b Why was it so against South Africa?

2 Re-read Source 6 above.
What kind of future does the Lusaka Manifesto suggest for white South Africans (Point 8)?

3 To what extent does the Lusaka Manifesto suggest that violence should be used against South Africa (Point 12)?

4 Re-read Source 7.
a What does Vorster mean by (i) 'war-mongering' and (ii) 'the white man ... is not expendable'?
b To what extent does the Lusaka Manifesto (i) 'war-monger' and (ii) suggest that the white man is expendable?

White South Africa defies world opinion

Events in Rhodesia (now Zimbabwe) and South-West Africa (now Namibia) made South Africa even less popular internationally, but the Nationalists refused to bend to world opinion.

How did events in Rhodesia and South-West Africa affect South Africa's relations with the rest of the world?

Rhodesia (Zimbabwe)

Background

Southern Rhodesia had become a British colony in 1890 when Cecil Rhodes' private army invaded the lands between the Limpopo and Zambezi rivers. Whites, mainly from Britain and South Africa, settled in the country. Most came to farm or to mine. In 1923 Britain gave them the choice of joining the Union of South Africa or becoming a separate, self-governing colony. They chose the latter. By the early 1960s, whites in Southern Rhodesia numbered about 240,000, the blacks about 4 million – that is, a ratio of one white to sixteen blacks.

In 1953, the British government joined together Northern Rhodesia, Southern Rhodesia and Nyasaland, to form the Central African Federation. However, the local black nationalist movements opposed federation and persuaded Britain to end it. Both Northern Rhodesia and Nyasaland gained their independence in 1964, the former as Zambia, the latter as Malawi. The blacks of Southern Rhodesia expected to gain their independence in the near future.

Source 1

The friendly buffer states on South Africa's borders, 1964–74.

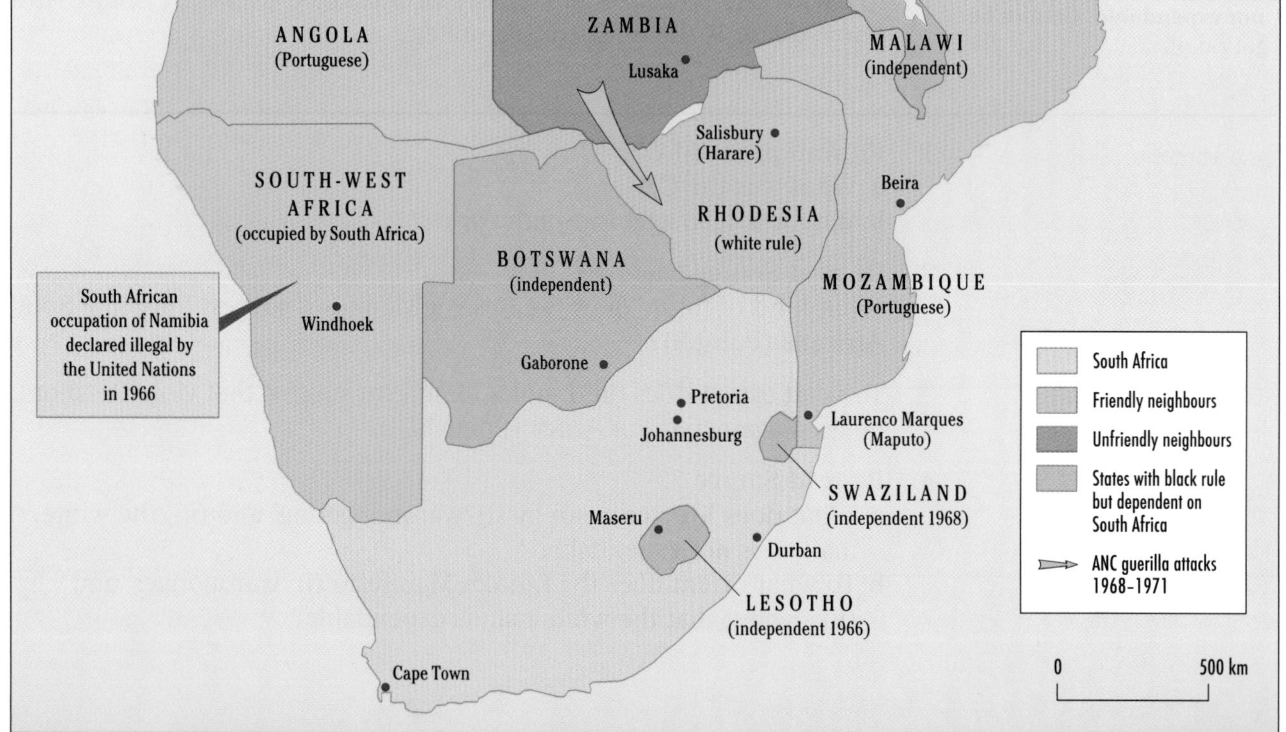

S.A. Cabinet is behind Rhodesia

SUNDAY TIMES REPORTER

THE South African Government is wholeheartedly behind the Prime Minister of Rhodesia, Mr. Ian Smith, in his dramatic bid this week for sovereign independence.

This was disclosed by the Minister of Transport, Mr. B. J. Schoeman, who said at a private meeting in Pretoria this week that the Government regarded Rhodesia as South Africa's "White frontier" on the Zambesi. In this situation, he said, Rhodesia's declaration of independence called for South Africa's complete support.

The Minister said said that if Rhodesia disappeared under Black rule, South Africa's frontier would be reduced to the line of the Limpopo.

"There may be serious repercussions as a result of Rhodesia's decision," he said, "but one must keep one's head."

Mr. Schoeman was talking to a deputation of the Federal Consultative Council of the Railways Staff Association, who had come to thank him for improvements in service conditions.

It was learnt later that a number of top railway officials left South Africa this week for top level talks with the Rhodesian railway authorities.

It is understood that their talks will be connected with the enormous expansion of railway traffic between South Africa and Rhodesia if South Africa becomes the only source of supply of Rhodesian imports in the event of international sanctions and boycotts.

One of the main subjects to be discussed is the laying of the line between Beit Bridge and West Nicholson.

This is regarded to be of major importance as the present rail link between South Africa and Rhodesia runs through Bechuanaland — still under British control.

Source 2

The South African Cabinet lines up behind Ian Smith. This headline from the South African *Sunday Times* is from immediately after UDI.

The Unilateral Declaration of Independence (UDI)

The white settlers of Southern Rhodesia, however, had other ideas. They were appalled by the move towards black rule. Not far away was what had been the Belgian Congo. In 1960, the Belgian government had given independence to an unprepared country and a dreadful civil war had followed. The Rhodesian whites believed that the same would happen if they handed power to the blacks. So when, in 1965, Britain's Labour government refused to give them independence unless they shared more of their political power with the black majority, Ian Smith, Rhodesia's Prime Minister, declared the country independent without Britain's consent. This event became known as UDI, the Unilateral Declaration of Independence.

Sanctions against Rhodesia

UDI shocked the rest of the world. Britain and the United Nations declared it to be illegal and recommended economic sanctions, including a ban on oil supplies. What South Africa decided to do was vital. Since most of Rhodesia's supplies came through South Africa, Smith would not survive if South Africa agreed to impose sanctions.

Source 1 gives a good idea of South Africa's position. Smith's government survived the next few years thanks largely to South African support. Many white South Africans had friends and relations in Rhodesia. Moreover, when they looked at the map, they saw that Rhodesia was a buffer between them and black Africa. Should Rhodesia fall, they were sure that they would be the next target of the black revolutionaries, who would be supported by the UN, the OAU and the forces of international communism.

So South Africa refused to have anything to do with economic sanctions against Rhodesia. Virtually everything that the Rhodesians needed, which they could not grow or make themselves, including oil, reached them through South Africa or the Portuguese colony of Mozambique. Vorster also sent South African police to help Smith in his struggle against the guerrilla forces of the black nationalist movement, who, for their part, had the backing of the ANC in exile.

South-West Africa (Namibia)

Background

South African behaviour in South-West Africa seemed to the rest of the world even more outrageous. The Germans had colonised the area between 1884 and 1914, but during the First World War, a South African army had defeated the Germans and taken control. In 1919, the new League of Nations gave South Africa the 'mandate' for South-West Africa. The 'mandate' theory was that, under the League's supervision, South Africa could run the country until its inhabitants were ready for independence. In reality, the South African government had treated South-West Africa like its own colony and had done nothing to prepare the black majority for independence.

The United Nations intervenes

At the end of the Second World War the United Nations replaced the League of Nations. Smuts then expected that the UN would allow South-West Africa to become fully part of South Africa. However, a strong Indian protest against Smuts' racial policies prevented such a development. Instead, the UN tried to make the South African government genuinely prepare the area for independence under UN supervision. This was the last thing that white South Africa could accept – an independent, black-ruled nation right next door! Instead, it put every obstacle possible in the way of UN involvement in the area while making it more and more part of South Africa proper. From 1949 the white inhabitants, who were mainly German or Afrikaners, were able to elect MPs to the South African Parliament and, in the 1960s, Verwoerd made clear his intention to introduce Bantustans there.

Between 1960 and 1966 Ethiopia and Liberia tried to persuade the International Court of Justice to rule that South Africa was not carrying out its responsibilities towards the inhabitants of South West Africa (Namibia). They failed, but in 1969 the UN declared that South African control of Namibia should end immediately. Vorster's policy was to keep talking to the UN but prevent any real progress towards black rule.

Black resistance in Namibia

For South Africa, the Namibian problem got steadily worse. Among the Ovambo people in the north a black resistance movement, the South-West African People's Organisation (SWAPO), had been founded in 1960. By the late 1960s it had much support and was capable of guerrilla war. The obvious problem for the UN was that, with Namibia entirely surrounded by white-run states, it could do little to aid SWAPO. What it did do in 1973 was to break off talks with the South African government and to declare SWAPO to be the true voice of the Namibian people.

True to form, the South African government treated SWAPO in the same way as the ANC, declaring it illegal and banning, imprisoning or driving its leaders into exile. Up to 1974, the South African Defence Force (SADF) succeeded in keeping Namibia under its control.

Questions

1. Draw a simple sketch map of central and southern Africa in 1970 to show the position of (a) Rhodesia (Zimbabwe) and (b) South-West Africa (Namibia) in relation to their neighbours. Make clear which states have black and which white governments.

2. Re-read pages 58–59 and study Source 1.
   a Why did South Africa support Smith's UDI in 1966?
   b How important to white Rhodesia was South African support between 1966 and 1974?

3. **a** Explain why the UN and the South African government came into conflict over Namibia.
   b What essentially was the aim of the South African government towards Namibia between 1948 and 1974?
   c What success did it have in those years?

White South Africa withstands the world

The world huffed and puffed, but the Nationalists continued their apartheid policies at home and defied the UN over Rhodesia and Namibia. They got away with their defiance and appeared to grow in confidence, thanks to their economic strength and the Cold War.

Source 1

Mineral production in South Africa, 1979. These figures were provided by the South African Ministry of Information.

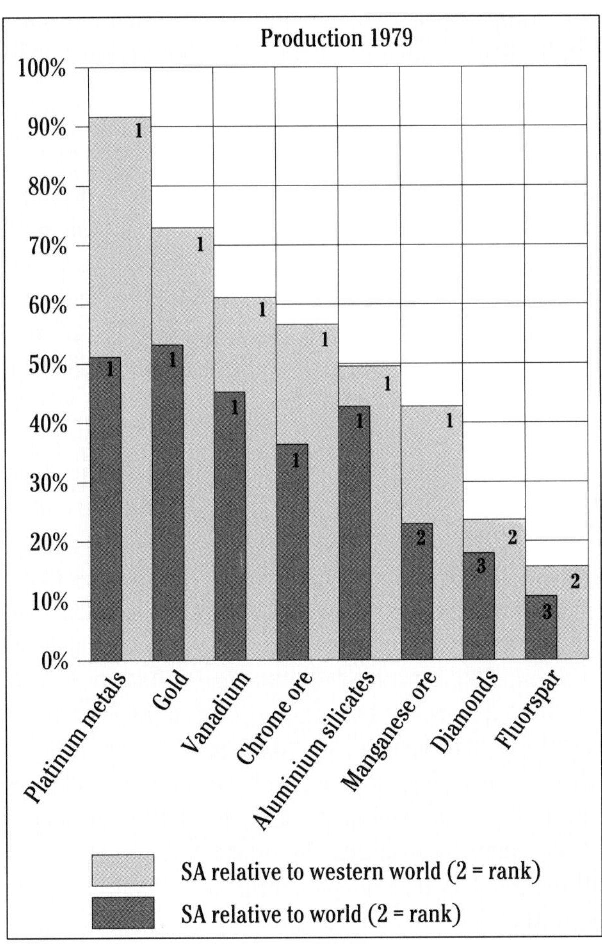

Why was the world unable to make South Africa change?

South Africa and the world economy

White South Africans could defy the rest of the world because they were economically strong. Between 1961 and 1970, their economy grew between 5 and 7 per cent each year, very fast by European standards. Business people all over the world wanted to share in this wealth so they put money in white South African businesses. The British were the largest investors, followed by the United States, West Germany and Japan.

In addition, South Africa possessed more valuable minerals than any country other than the Soviet Union (see Source 1). New gold-fields were discovered in the Orange Free State and more diamonds were found in South-West Africa. But this was only part of the story. South Africa was the major producer of a number of rare minerals. Source 2 explains how some of these were vital to American and European industries.

Source 2

Arnt Spandau, *Southern Africa and the Western World*, 1984.

For some strategic metals, there are no substitutes at any price. Industrialised countries must have them or write off a good part of their technological advance. The most critical of all industrial metals, known as the 'Big Four', are chromium, cobalt, manganese and the platinum group metals. As one steel executive recently [1981] put it: 'Without these [Big Four] you couldn't build a jet engine or an automobile, run a train, build an oil refinery or a power plant. You couldn't process food, or run a sanitary restaurant or a hospital operating room. You could not build a computer ....'

Consequently, however much American and European companies and governments said that they disliked apartheid, they would not back schemes put forward by the UN or the OAU to overthrow the white government. They themselves had too much to lose in investments and in vital mineral supplies. Many of them argued that the richer South Africa grew, the better-off the blacks would become. Slowly but surely, they said, white governments would listen more carefully to business leaders and gradually bring to an end the apartheid system.

The southern African economy

South Africa was also able to ignore the criticisms of its immediate neighbours because it had an economic stranglehold on them. The mines provided desperately needed work for blacks who migrated from Mozambique, Botswana and Lesotho. In addition, most of the important road and rail routes, along which the vital exports of its neighbours had to pass, went through South Africa to its ports of Durban and Cape Town (see page 10).

Economic success meant that the government could spend money on its armed forces. As a result, white South Africa had by far the strongest army and air force in the region and made sure that they were armed with up-to-date weapons.

South Africa and the Cold War

The global Cold War between the two superpowers, the capitalist United States and the West against communist Soviet Union and the East, was another important reason why white South Africa was able to ignore the anger of the UN. Both superpowers wanted to strengthen their positions in Africa. Whatever Britain and the United States might say about the horrors of apartheid, when it came to the crunch, they believed that they needed white South Africa too much in their struggle against world communism to let it be seriously threatened.

White South Africans were strongly capitalist. They believed in free enterprise, private property and low taxes. Moreover, American and European business needed South Africa, especially its minerals (see Sources 1 and 2 above). Geographically, South Africa seemed important in the Cold War since it commanded a vital sea route, that taken by tankers carrying oil – the essential fuel of modern industry – from the Persian Gulf to the West. Under no circumstances would America and Britain allow South Africa to fall under the control of a government which was more friendly to the Soviet Union than to them.

Within South Africa, the Nationalists convinced themselves that a communist-inspired onslaught was directed against them, and used every opportunity to tell their citizens and the outside world how dangerous the Communists were and how only the Nationalists could be trusted to keep South Africa safely part of the freedom-loving capitalist West. P. W. Botha, Minister of Defence, made clear the government's thinking about the Soviet Union, in a speech in 1977:

Source 3

Quoted by A. Starke in *Survival*, 1978.

There is no doubt in my mind that Russia is the dominating force in international affairs today. So politically, economically and as far as relationships between people are concerned, very much depends on how successful Russia is in her expansionary total-war effort. In the first instance she is out to dominate Europe.... She will only try to use force when she doesn't succeed in intimidating [frightening] enough

European countries far enough, and it looks like the latter is working.

Secondly she wants to control the destiny of Africa, for its raw materials and the sea route round the Cape – Russia is expanding her navy faster than any country in history and that can only mean that she wants to dominate the seas. If you want to dominate the seas, you must be able to control the South Atlantic and the Indian Ocean.

The moment she succeeds in either the one or the other, Russia will concentrate on isolating America from Europe.

The Department of Foreign Affairs and Information neatly linked South Africa's mineral riches and the Cold War in a pamphlet published in 1982 called 'The Vital Role of South Africa's Minerals' (Sources 4 and 5).

Source 4

Destination of South Africa's mineral exports, 1979. From 'The Vital Role of South Africa's Minerals', 1982.

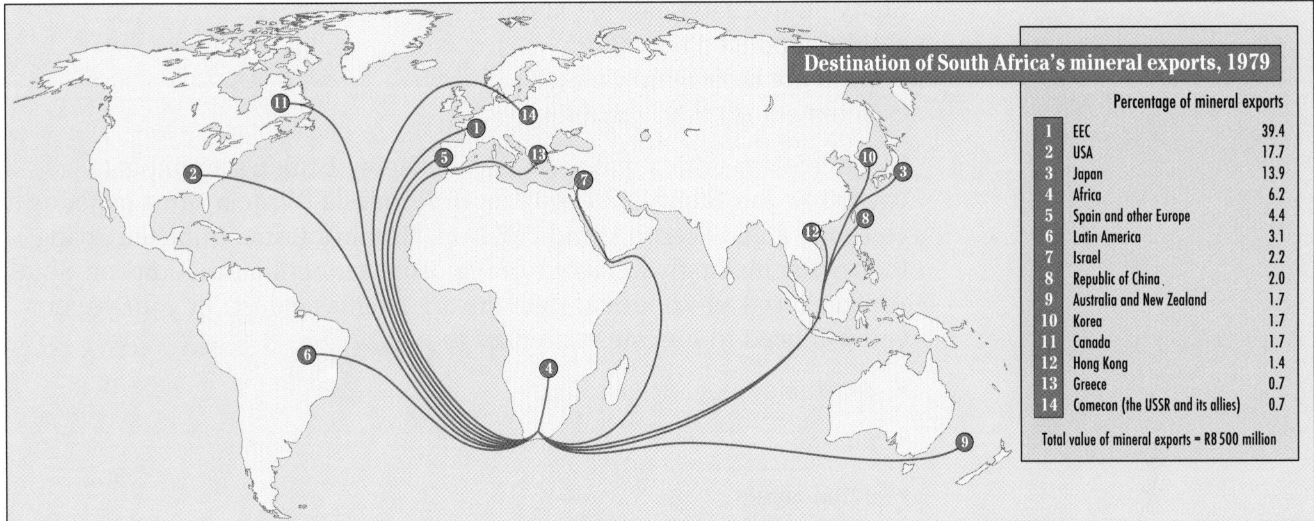

Source 5

'The Vital Role of South Africa's Minerals', published by the South African Ministry of Information, 1982.

In view of the dependence of the West on supplies of strategic minerals from South Africa ... it would surely not be an exaggeration to suggest that should a Soviet puppet regime* ever be installed in Pretoria ... the Soviet Union would by this action grasp the perfect instrument for ... destroying the industrial and technological supremacy of the West.

* **Soviet puppet regime** A black government which took orders from the Soviet Union.

Questions

Study sources 3, 4 and 5 and re-read pages 61–63.

1 **a** For what reasons does P. W. Botha (Source 3) think the Soviet Union dangerous?

b Why do you think he specifically mentions the sea route round the Cape?

2 Source 4 comes from a pamphlet given out by the South African Embassy in London. What is the message of the diagram?

3 How did South Africa's economic strength help it to ignore international criticisms?

Unit 4 Review

Questions

1 Study pages 55–56.
- **a** What did Macmillan mean by 'the wind of change'?
- **b** What changes did black nationalists want in South Africa?
- **c** When and why did South Africa leave the British Commonwealth?
- **d** What did Verwoerd mean when he said: 'We have nowhere else to go.'

2 Study pages 56–60.
- **a** In 1970 which countries acted as buffers between South Africa and independent black nations?
- **b** What did South Africa do for Rhodesia and in Namibia to anger the United Nations?

3 Study Source 1 on page 61 and Source 4 on page 63.
- **a** Who produced them?
- **b** What are their main points?
- **c** Comment on their reliability.

4 In 1969 South Africa was seriously damaging Britain's attempts to overthrow Ian Smith's government in Rhodesia. Write a short paper as if you were an adviser to Harold Wilson, Britain's Prime Minister, giving the arguments firstly in favour of imposing economic sanctions on South Africa as well as Rhodesia, then the arguments against. In your paper you will need to include references to

- apartheid;
- racism;
- equal rights;
- world opinion;
- business links;
- profits;
- vital minerals;
- the oil route to the Middle East;
- the Communist threat.

Unit 5 · Economic and social trends, 1960–90

Economic trends

As Sources 1 and 2 show, the South African economy grew fast through the 1960s and 1970s but slowed down in the 1980s. In the late 1980s it ran into its first serious depression since the 1930s. At the same time the population was growing ever faster, so the economic slow-down had serious social and political consequences.

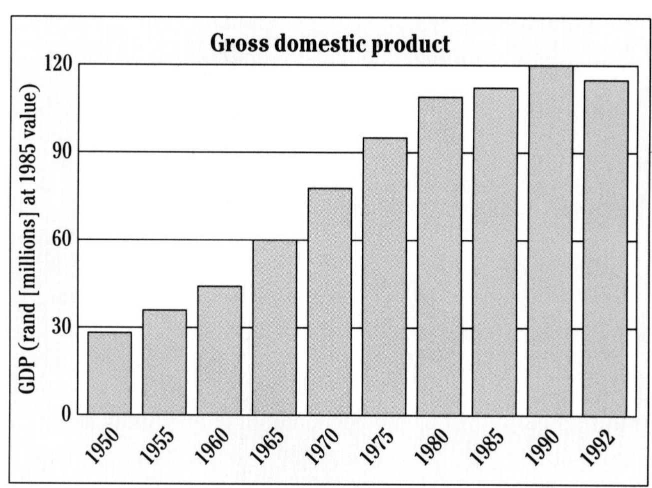

Source 1

South Africa's Gross Domestic Product (GDP), 1950–92. GDP is the total value of the goods and services produced each year by the country. Economists use this as a measure of a country's wealth.

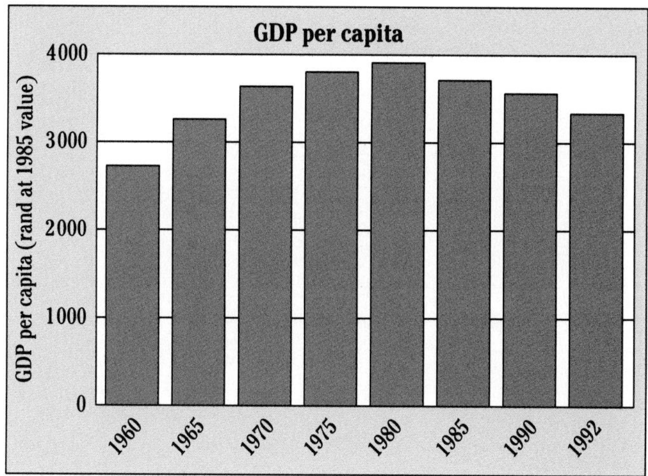

Source 2

South Africa's GDP per capita. This is the GDP divided by the number of inhabitants to show their average wealth.

Why and with what results did the economy grow and then slow down?

Minerals and manufacturing

Minerals (see pages 12–13) were one reason for the rapid growth of the early years. Another was manufacturing. Gold usually meant that bad times for the rest of the world were usually good for South Africa. For example, during the international oil crisis of 1973, the price of gold soared to $800 per ounce, which meant huge profits for the mining companies. Between 1951 and 1971 the number of people employed in manufacturing doubled. Heavy industry (such as steel or car assembly)

Source 3
Booming Johannesburg in the 1970s.

linked the advanced technology and business methods of the United States and Europe with cheap, black labour costs, and consequently made good profits.

The Anglo-American Corporation

Large companies were typical of South African business. Much the largest was the Anglo-American Corporation, which had been created by Sir Ernest Oppenheimer in the 1920s and 1930s. Oppenheimer had taken control of Cecil Rhodes' old diamond company, De Beers, and amalgamated it with other mines on the Rand and in Central Africa. When he died in 1957, he was one of the richest men in the world. Under the leadership of his son Harry, 'Anglo' moved into many other fields, including chemicals, banking and newspapers. It was said in the late 1970s that 50 per cent of the shares traded in the Johannesburg Stock Market were owned by 'Anglo' companies.

The government and the economy

The other big business element was the government. The state owned the railways, the electricity and water industry. It was a major steel producer. It also invested heavily in coal-into-oil plants like the one shown in Source 4. It feared that its international enemies might organise a trade war and have as their most dangerous weapon the cutting off of oil supplies, and South Africa had large coal reserves but no oil.

For similar reasons, the government created a large arms industry. In 1966 70 per cent of arms was imported, but by 1982 80 per cent of a much larger amount was locally made. Armscor, the state-owned armaments company, also became an exporter. It was aided by European and Israeli advisers (the South African Air Force flew French-designed Mirage and Italian-designed Impala aircraft). Nuclear weapons were also developed secretly, with French assistance.

The government also invested in major road-building projects and in ambitious irrigation schemes like the Hendrik Verwoerd dam.

Source 4

Refineries at Sasolburg converted South Africa's abundant coal into vital oil. *SA Handbook,* 1985.

White people and the economy

The people who benefitted most from this growth were the whites, particularly the Afrikaners. Traditionally, the English-speaking whites had run South African business and, in 1948 they earned twice as much per head as Afrikaners. By the late 1970s, however, most Afrikaners had become city-dwellers; large, successful Afrikaner companies had appeared (such as Anton Rupert's Rembrandt tobacco company), and, during a period when white incomes had risen sharply anyway, had come to earn 80 per cent of the average English-speakers' income.

Black people and the economy

Black incomes seem hardly to have risen at all between 1948 and 1970. However, after 1970 the incomes of many blacks rose considerably. This was due partly to effective trade-union action, partly to international criticism of low black wages in comparison to white wealth, and partly to the belief of both employers and the government that they would benefit by creating a class of better-paid, skilled black workers. Between 1970 and 1986 real wages for blacks in manufacturing and building rose by 60 per cent while whites' wages rose by only 18 per cent. The major problem of the 1980s and 1990s was high black unemployment and large pockets of severe poverty due to 'forced removals' (see pages 72–75).

The economic slow-down

The economy slowed down for a number of reasons in the 1980s: trade boycotts, threats of international sanctions and serious political and social unrest (see pages 85–89). Another important reason was the effects of apartheid. Harry Oppenheimer warned in 1971:

Source 5

Quoted in *The Legacy of Apartheid*, (publisher The Guardian) 1994.

> Prospects for economic growth will not be attained so long as a large majority of the population is prevented by lack of formal education and technical training or by positive prohibition [e.g. the apartheid laws affecting black employment] from playing a full part of which it is capable in the national development.

Questions

Re-read pages 65–68.

1 What were the main reasons for:
a the country's economic growth up to 1980, and
b the slow-down after 1980?

2 How did the groups below do economically between 1948 and 1984?
a the Afrikaners;
b the urban blacks.

3 What apartheid laws might Oppenheimer have had in mind in Source 5?

Social trends

South African society was exceptionally divided, not just between whites and blacks but also within the colour boundaries. The ruling group, the Afrikaners, were especially isolated from the outside world. Growing wealth lessened that isolation and caused more whites to look critically at apartheid. The main trend for blacks was to move to cities, where they became better educated and less ready to tolerate the burdens of apartheid.

The main features of South African society

White society

Visitors to South Africa from abroad were immediately struck by the lack of contact between the different peoples. As a first impression the Afrikaans/English-speaking split between the whites was as striking as that between blacks and whites. White South Africans spoke different languages, their children attended different schools and they generally lived in different suburbs. Allister Sparks, a leading journalist, describes how he once addressed a group of 300 English-speaking schoolchildren in Johannesburg:

Source 1

Allister Sparks, *The Mind of South Africa*, 1990.

I asked how many knew an Afrikaner child of roughly the same age whom they could loosely describe as a friend. Five put up their hands. When I asked how many knew a black child outside the master–servant relationship, there were three hands.

As for the average white's understanding of the blacks, it was usually clouded both by distance and by the master–servant relationship. Rian Malan, who grew up in an Afrikaner suburb of Johannesburg, recalls his first memories of blacks:

Source 2

Rian Malan, *My Traitor's Heart*, 1990.

There were always Africans in our backyard. We called them natives. They lived in cold, dark rooms with tiny windows .... Natives cooked my meals, polished my shoes, made my bed, mowed the lawn, trimmed the hedge, and dug holes at my father's direction. They ate on enamel plates and drank out of chipped cups with no handles, which was known as the boy's cup or girl's cup and kept separate from the rest of our china. They spoke broken English or Afrikaans, wore old clothes, had no money and no last names. That was all it was really necessary to know about them.

With rising incomes, spacious homes and gardens (normally with a swimming pool), a ready supply of servants and a fine climate, white South Africans had a lifestyle which was frequently described as 'Californian'. There was certainly an American feel to it with its high car ownership and much of its culture – from advertising to the cinema – was influenced by the United States. British influences, too, were strong, since most of the English-speakers, unlike the Afrikaners, still had close family links with Europe.

However, white South Africans were culturally isolated. The government banned television until 1976 and controlled the radio. Few Afrikaners travelled overseas. There was a recognisably South African white culture: male, smoking, drinking and sports-mad. Rugby was the religion, followed by cricket, golf and tennis. There was a 1960s advertisement for Chevrolet cars which summed it up in six words: 'Braaivleis [barbecue], Rugby, Sunny Skies and Chevrolet'.

During the 1970s this cultural isolation lessened. Wealth and education encouraged whites to both travel more and think harder. The government allowed television from 1976. Though feminism was not an obviously strong movement, many South African women were well educated, independent and unafraid of responsible jobs. Divorce rates soared and a less male-dominated culture emerged.

Among English-speaking whites, there was a long liberal tradition strongly critical of the government. It came through newspapers like the *Cape Times* and the *Rand Daily Mail*; through political parties like the Liberals and Progressives; through the churches like the Anglicans, who elected Desmond Tutu to be the first black Archbishop of Cape Town; through research institutes like the South African Institute of Race Relations, and through novelists like Nadine Gordimer.

The Afrikaners also had their own powerful critics of apartheid: Beyers Naude, a former minister of the Dutch Reformed Church who left to found the Christian Institute; the Sestiger (Sixties) group of writers; the novelists like J. M. Coetzee and André Brink. By the late 1970s, Afrikaners were divided in their attitudes to apartheid between the 'verligtes' (enlightened) who were ready to consider change and the 'verkramptes' (narrow) who held on rigidly to the Verwoerdian grand design.

Black society

Most blacks vividly remembered early experiences of white habits of assumed superiority. Mandela tells how at the age of ninteen (in the 1930s) he and Paul Mathabane, a university friend, were on holiday, standing outside the post office at Umtata.

Source 3

Nelson Mandela, *Long Walk to Freedom*, 1994.

The local magistrate, a white man in his sixties, approached Paul and asked him to go inside and buy him some postage stamps. It was quite common for any white person to call on any black person to perform a chore. (Paul refused.) The magistrate was offended. 'Do you know who I am?' he said, his face turning red with irritation. 'It is not necessary to know who you are,' Mathabane said. 'I know what you are.' The magistrate asked him what exactly he meant by that. 'I mean that you are a rogue!' Paul said heatedly. The magistrate boiled over and exclaimed, 'You'll pay dearly for this!' and walked away.

Things had not changed much by 1976 when Frank Chikane was training to be a priest and shared an office with some white Christian youth workers. They kept a tin mug for him while everyone else had china.

Source 4

Frank Chikane, *No Life of My Own*, 1988.

> The next thing that happened was that I was told not to use the toilet just next to my office, but the one on the top floor.... I continued to use it. Then a special delegation was sent to tell me that these fellow 'Christians' were upset that I continued to use the toilet when they had asked me not to.... Then a lock was put on the toilet and all those with white skins were given duplicates of the key.

As time passed fewer blacks were prepared to go on suffering such humiliations in silence. More were employed in settled jobs in the cities which required education and skills – clerks, civil servants, teachers, nurses, business people (especially building and taxi firms). They knew that they were the equal of whites.

These were the black elite. They would live in the most pleasant parts of the townships – for example, Lamontville, near Durban. They might well own a car. They would drink lager or wine rather than Bantu beer. Church membership was important, especially for the women, and choirs linked to institutions like churches, hospitals and schools were popular. Another important social institution was the 'stokvel' – a method of collective saving. A group would pool their savings so that each member could afford a large one-off payment when necessary (such as the funeral costs of a relative).

Black society had its divisions too. Semi-skilled urban workers also increased both in numbers and in wealth. Among them American/West Indian influences were strong, like Bob Marley and reggae music in the 1970s. Soccer rather than Rugby was their passion.

And then there were millions of others, struggling simply to survive. Many worked in white homes as maids or garden 'boys'. The mines and their male-only compounds (see page 14) remained big employers. The fortunes of many families rose and fell depending on whether jobs were available or whether wage-earners lost their jobs because of the pass laws. Mark Mathabane, whose father was put in prison for pass law offences (see page 50), remembers having to go out to the Alexandra township garbage dump in search of food in the 1960s:

Source 5

M. Mathabane, *Kaffir Boy*, 1988.

> Every weekday huge, grey trucks arrived to dump garbage from white people's homes. Each morning, my mother would take Florah, George and me and the four of us would join the throng of black men, women and children flocking down there. We always left home between six and seven in the morning so we could be in the first wave of people rushing to the trucks as they came in, usually around ten.

Mathabane also remembers the 'tsotsis', the terrifying young gangsters who terrorised the townships, and other gangs of criminals who, through protection rackets, sometimes had more control of an area than the police. Slums, overcrowding, unemployment, poverty and despair all helped to create a violent, large and growing criminal element in the townships.

Source 6

Murder on the Cape Flats, 1979.

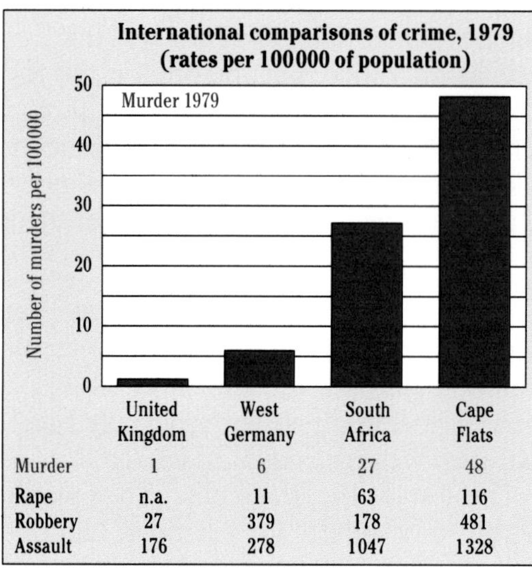

	United Kingdom	West Germany	South Africa	Cape Flats
Murder	1	6	27	48
Rape	n.a.	11	63	116
Robbery	27	379	178	481
Assault	176	278	1047	1328

Another source of violence was the growing tension between those blacks who were totally settled in towns with their urban culture, and those who respected their rural roots. This exploded into appalling violence in the 1980s and early 1990s (see pages 99–100 and pages 119-120).

Questions

Re-read pages 69–72.

1 Explain the terms: braaivleis, Sestiger, liberal, verkrampte, verligte, elite, stokvel, tsotsis.

2 For what reasons were Afrikaners less isolated in the 1980s than they had been in the 1960s?

3 Most white South Africans had a good life in the 1960s and knew it. What were the main characteristics of this good life?

4 Who made up the black elite? What were the main characteristics of their life?

5 There was a lot of violence in the townships. Where did it come from?

The dispossessed people

The full effect of Verwoerd's ideas on separate development did not appear until the 1970s and 1980s. An enormous, government-enforced movement of black people took place at a time when more whites were beginning to realise that 'separate development' could never work.

Why and with what results were so many blacks moved from their homes?

Source 1 shows how the rise in the numbers of blacks accelerated from the late 1950s. Simultaneously, the government was moving blacks from the cities by the Group Areas Act. It was also out to destroy 'black spots'

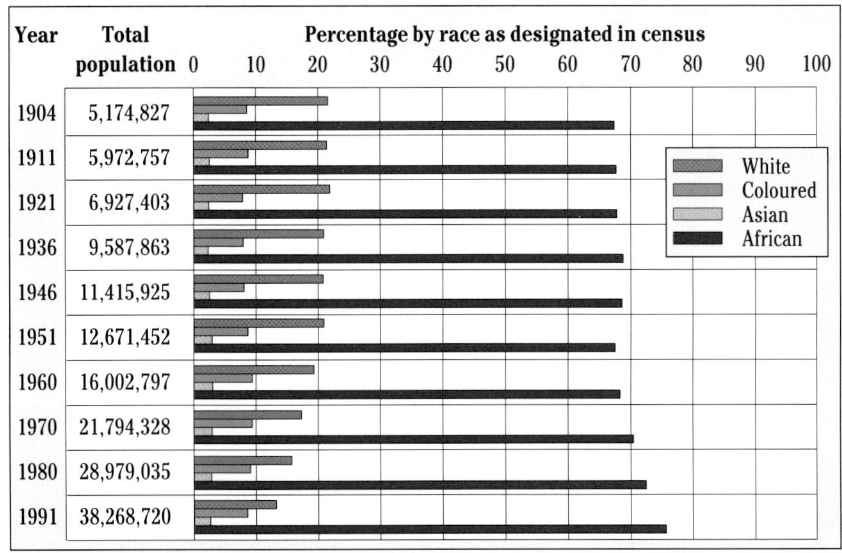

Source 1

The population of South Africa, 1904–91.

(those places in 'white' rural areas where blacks still lived). Unfortunately, at the same time, white farmers, who, up to 1970, had been much the largest employers of blacks, cut their workforces drastically. They did this by introducing machinery and changing from pastoral to arable farming. The consequences of these changes were the forced movement from their homes of more than two million blacks, even greater poverty, enormous suffering and anger which, in the 1980s, spilled over into violent politics (see Units 7 and 8).

Example 1: Welcome Valley resettlement camp

In Verwoerd's vision of separate development, the government would provide for the basic needs of the resettled blacks. The blacks, delighted to return to their fertile, productive homelands, would quickly build their own houses and develop their own way of life unspoilt by the evils of the white cities. The reality was very different, as Cosmos Desmond, a Catholic priest, brought vividly to the notice of the world in 1971.

Source 2

Cosmos Desmond, *The Discarded People*, 1971.

... not enough water and not enough land even for subsistence farming. There is no industry and no work within daily reach. The inhabitants struggle against disease on the edge of starvation. It is impossible to say whether the physical degradation or the mental torture of living in such a place is the more terrible.

Source 3

Corrugated iron toilets and little else await their forcibly removed owners. The Welcome Valley resettlement camp in 1968.

Example 2: Unibel

Unibel was a squatter camp of 25,000 people on the Cape Flats near Cape Town. Its inhabitants were there because they had nowhere else to go. There was no employment in the countryside. The only possible source of work was Cape Town. Government policy, however, was that they should move to the Ciskei Bantustan, hundreds of kilometres away. Yet even after bulldozers had destroyed their homes, only a few accepted the government's offer of free transport to unemployment in Ciskei. The rest disappeared into the much larger Crossroads squatter camp nearby, to live through more years of harassment and violence but at least some chance of paid work.

Source 4

A government bulldozer crushes the Unibel squatter camp, 1978.

Example 3: Glenmore

Jamangile Tsotsobe lived at Colchester, near Port Elizabeth, with his wife and epileptic granddaughter. He had lived there for thirty years and worked as a gardener. Life was fairly good. They had enough to eat and plenty of friends and neighbours. However, in 1979, the Bantu Affairs Administration Board (Baab) decided that they were squatters in a white area and forced them to move to a relocation camp in Glenmore, 200 kilometres away.

Source 5

Laurine Platzky and Cherryl Walker, *The Surplus People*, 1985. The Surplus People Project investigated the effect of these forced removals in detail. Some of its project workers were arrested by the police and two were detained for ten months.

They were told that there would be work for everybody and there were good houses which they could have for free ... but they did not want to move. They were happy enough where they were.... They knew that Baab would never give a black man a house for free.... Suddenly they were given seven days notice to leave ... the trucks came very early when they were asleep ... the officials were angry men who shouted to them to get out ... the houses were demolished before they could get their belongings out ... their furniture was broken. The houses in Glenmore were bare, with draughty wooden walls they had to fix with mud. Tsotsobe looks at us and says that now there is no hope. When he was young, he wanted to give to his children and grandchildren a different kind of life. Now he sees that there is no hope for his children.

The townships

The government's first response to the black surge towards the cities was to enforce even more firmly the controls which already existed through the pass laws. When such measures were clearly not enough, they redrew the boundaries of some Bantustans to include townships not far from white factories so that blacks could commute to work yet live in a homeland. Umlazi, for example, formerly part of Durban, became part of KwaZulu, and Mdantsane, near East London, was taken over by the Ciskei.

Source 6

Commuting for hours to work in Pretoria.

Some of these townships grew at an amazing pace. Botshabelo, 50 kilometres from Bloemfontein, grew from 100,000 in 1980 to well over 300,000 in 1985. Most work was either in Bloemfontein (a 50-kilometre journey by bus) or further away on the mines. Other 'commuters' were the Kwandebele, whose settlement of 300,000 was heavily dependent in the 1980s on work in Pretoria, 100 kilometres away. The Putco bus firm ran 250 buses per day on which some workers would have to travel up to six hours daily. An American journalist described the Kwandebele as 'a nation of sleep-walkers'.

The pressure of numbers

As well as forcing people into these huge, artificial townships and squatter camps, apartheid policies so crowded the Bantustans that the land could not cope with the weight of population. People ate less well and few townships had electricity or supplied water to each of its houses. Coal was expensive so people had to use wood for fuel.

Source 7

F. Wilson and M. Ramphele, *Uprooting Poverty: the South African challenge*, 1989.

One of the clearest images of the poverty in the country is the sight of a group of elderly black women, each carrying home on her head a load of firewood weighing up to 50 kg, passing under the high tension cables that carry the electric energy between the towns (and farmsteads) of the Republic.

Source 8

Carrying firewood home. Welcome Valley, 1970s.

Government excuses

Not until the late 1980s did the government begin to reconsider its policy of forced removals. Until then, it continued to try to justify its policies even when the hardship and suffering of those forced from their homes were well known. Source 9 is an example of how the government tried to justify its policy.

Source 9

Letter of J. J. C. Wentzel, Deputy Minister of Development and Land Affairs, to Mr Msibi, Chairman of the Driefontein Community Board, 18 December 1981.

The removal ... of so-called 'Black spots' ... is carried out in accordance with a policy which has as its goal the improvement of the standard of life of all people of South Africa.... It sometimes becomes necessary for people to be encouraged to move for their own good....

It is certainly not part of declared policy that people should be forced to move without consideration of their residential and other rights, nor that they should be exposed to hardship....

There are many Whites who also have had to leave land they have owned for generations.... Everyone of us has to make sacrifices in some way or other to further the peace and prosperity of this beautiful country of ours....

The relocation of your people will have to be carried out in the interests of all concerned.

Questions

1 Re-read pages 72–77 and Source 9. Then explain:
   a why J. J. C. Wentzel could believe that the removal of 'black spots' could be in the interests of all South Africans;
   b how he might have tried to counter the argument that all removals meant hardship for blacks.

2 It could be that Wentzel may have had some private worries about the forced removals policies. What might these worries have been?

Unit 5 Review

Questions

1 It is hard for visitors to judge a society on only a brief stay. How would you expect a fair-minded visitor interested in political and social trends to sum up the situation in your country after a month's touring, reading the newspapers and watching television?

2 This chapter contains a range of sources. How reliable would you expect the following to be:
   a Rian Malan (page 69) on white attitudes to blacks;
   b Nelson Mandela (page 70) and Frank Chikane (page 71) on their early memories of white superiority;
   c The Surplus People Project and witnesses like Tsotsobe (page 75) on forced removals?

3 Comment on the statement that 'between 1969 and 1990 many blacks did well and some whites suffered badly under the rule of the Nationalist government'.

Part 4: The collapse of apartheid
Unit 6 · Crisis years, 1973–77

White rule in South Africa was severely weakened in the mid-1970s by events both outside and inside the country. Outside, black governments, first in Angola and Mozambique, then in Zimbabwe (Rhodesia), took over from white ones. Internally, black resistance took on three new forms – trade-union action, 'Black Consciousness', and mass rioting by young people.

White power ends in the Portuguese Empire and Rhodesia

A revolution in Portugal in 1974 led directly to independence for the Portuguese African colonies. In Mozambique, a black government came to power, led by Samora Machel. In Angola a civil war broke out in which South Africa supported UNITA. In Rhodesia guerrilla war wore down the white Rhodesians, and Robert Mugabe's ZANU Party came to power. These changes posed many difficulties for white South Africa.

What were the consequences of this collapse?

You can see from Source 1 on page 79 that in 1970 South Africa had a buffer of friendly neighbours: the Portuguese colonies of Angola and Mozambique, and Ian Smith's Rhodesia. Botswana, though ruled by a black government, had too small a population and was economically too dependent on South Africa to be unfriendly. This buffer provided good protection against OAU enemies like Zambia and Tanzania and the ANC in exile.

The collapse of the Portuguese Empire
Source 2 on page 79 shows that by 1980 this buffer had gone forever. The Portuguese dictator Salazar and his successor, Caetano, had not accepted that a wind of change was blowing through Africa and they wasted money and lives in unwinnable and unpopular wars trying to save their African colonies. The army officers who overthrew Caetano in 1974 immediately granted independence to Angola and to Mozambique.

Angola, 1974–75
Angola quickly descended into chaos as three separate black nationalist movements fought one another to succeed the Portuguese: the Popular Front for the Liberation of Angola (MPLA), the National Front for the Liberation of Angola (FNLA) whose support lay mainly in the north of the country, and the National Union for the Total Independence of Angola (UNITA) whose support was mainly in the south.

ANGOLA
(Portuguese)
ZAMBIA
Lusaka
MALAWI
(independent)
Salisbury
(Harare)
SOUTH-WEST AFRICA
(occupied by South Africa)
Beira
RHODESIA
(white rule)
BOTSWANA
(independent)
MOZAMBIQUE
(Portuguese)
South African occupation of Namibia declared illegal by the United Nations in 1966
Windhoek
Gaborone
Pretoria
Johannesburg
Laurenco Marques
(Maputo)
SWAZILAND
(independent 1968)
Maseru
Durban
LESOTHO
(independent 1966)
Cape Town
South Africa
Friendly neighbours
Unfriendly neighbours
States with black rule but dependent on South Africa
ANC guerilla attacks 1968-1971
0
500 km

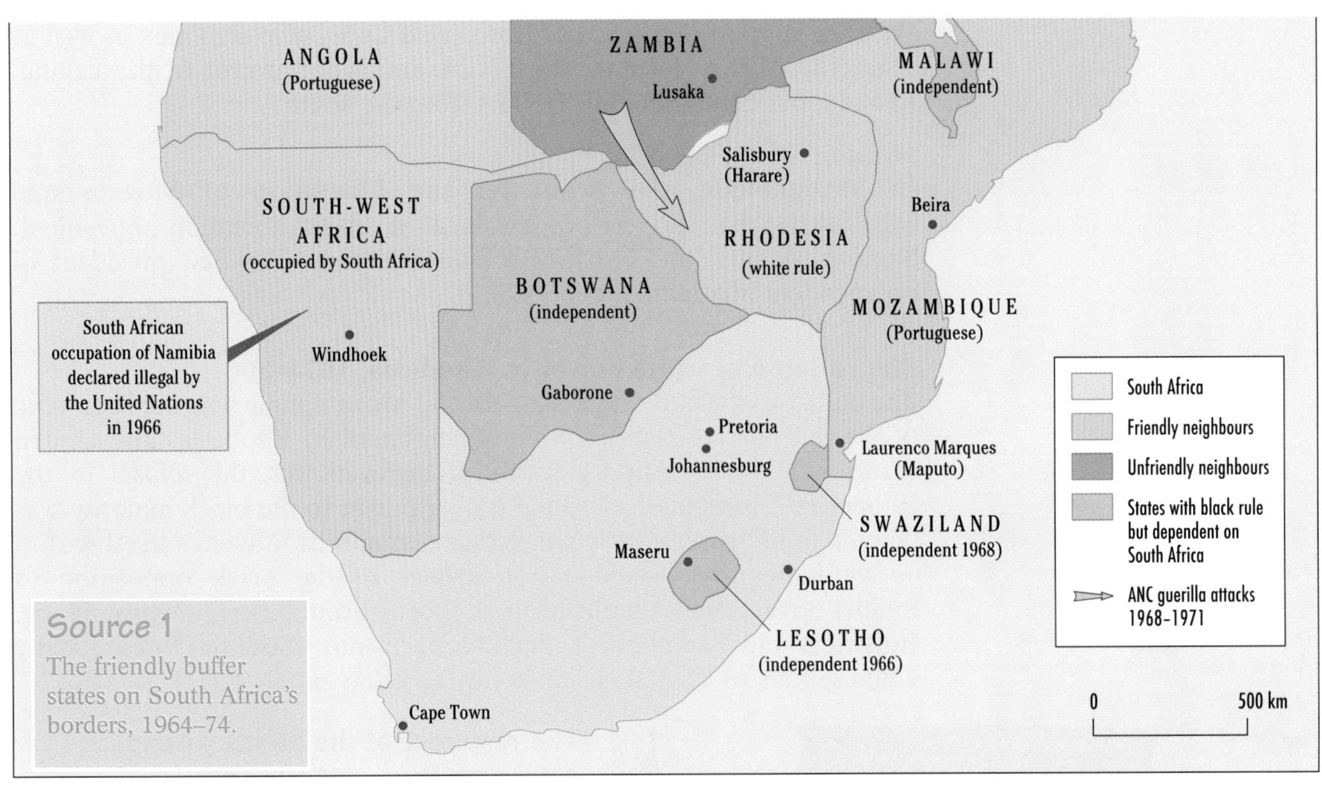

Source 1
The friendly buffer states on South Africa's borders, 1964–74.

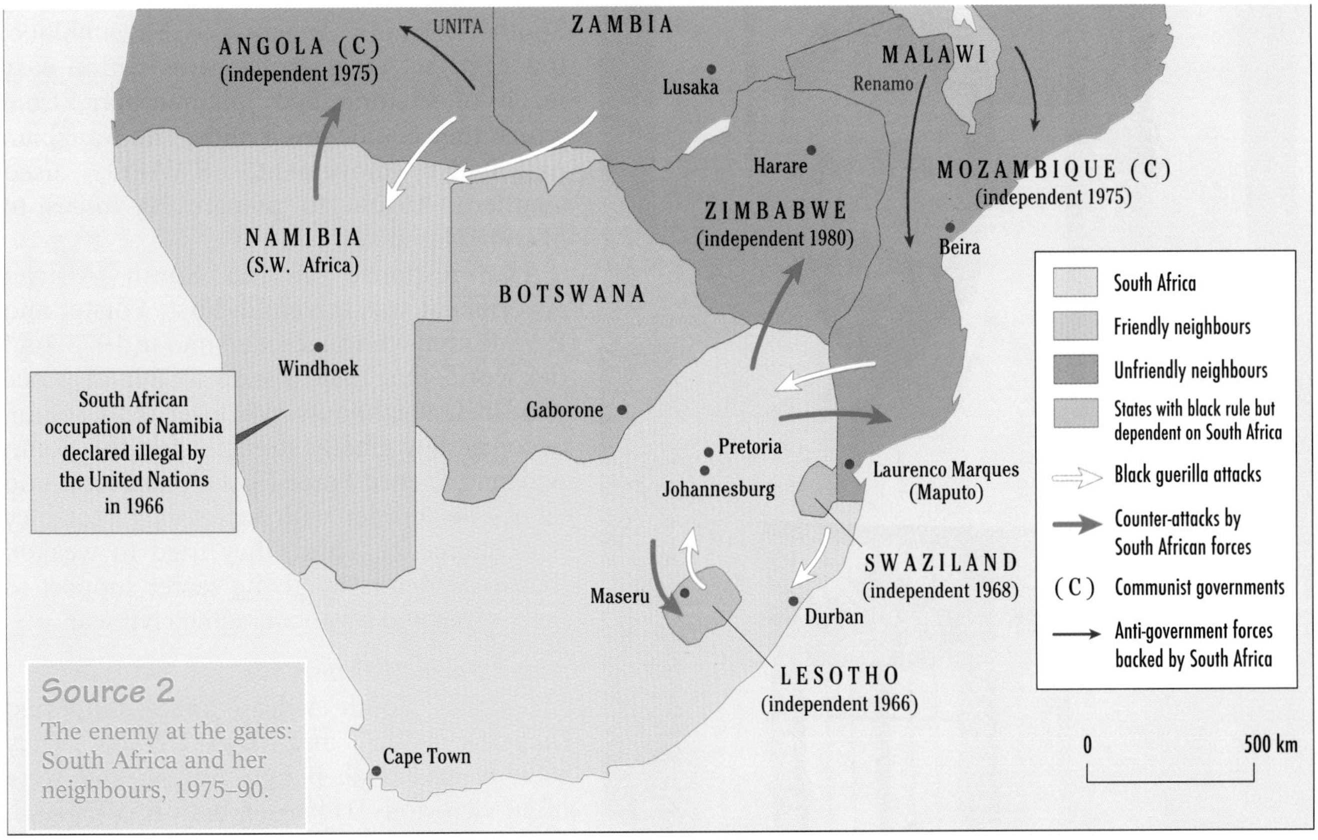

UNITA
ZAMBIA
ANGOLA (C)
(independent 1975)
Lusaka
MALAWI
Renamo
Harare
MOZAMBIQUE (C)
(independent 1975)
ZIMBABWE
(independent 1980)
NAMIBIA
(S.W. Africa)
Beira
BOTSWANA
Windhoek
South African occupation of Namibia declared illegal by the United Nations in 1966
Gaborone
Pretoria
Johannesburg
Laurenco Marques
(Maputo)
SWAZILAND
(independent 1968)
Maseru
Durban
LESOTHO
(independent 1966)
Cape Town
South Africa
Friendly neighbours
Unfriendly neighbours
States with black rule but dependent on South Africa
Black guerilla attacks
Counter-attacks by South African forces
(C) Communist governments
Anti-government forces backed by South Africa
0
500 km

Source 2
The enemy at the gates: South Africa and her neighbours, 1975–90.

With the support of the Soviet Union and Cuba, who sent men as well as arms, the MPLA defeated the FNLA and won control of the capital, Luanda, but could not shift UNITA from the south.

Mozambique, 1974–75

In Mozambique, the Front for the Liberation of Mozambique (FRELIMO) had no serious rivals as a black liberation movement. Samora Machel, the FRELIMO leader, became the first president of independent Mozambique in 1975.

The collapse of white power in Rhodesia, 1974–80

The collapse of white rule in Angola and Mozambique was the beginning of the end for Ian Smith's white government in Rhodesia. The United States would not support Smith. It believed that the refusal of the Rhodesian white minority to hand over power to the black majority was helping to increase rather than reduce communist influence in Africa.

Simultaneously, the liberation armies of the black opposition to Smith's government redoubled their efforts. From bases in Mozambique, Botswana and Zambia they attacked deep into Rhodesia, forcing many white settlers to leave their farms for the safety of the cities.

Source 3

The victorious Machel, underneath a huge portrait of himself, addresses his supporters in Maputo, Mozambique 1975.

The response of the South African government

These changes were very serious for white South Africa. In Angola and Mozambique, the ANC set up guerrilla bases within easy reach of Pretoria and Johannesburg, from which they could mount raids. The Namibian nationalist movement, SWAPO, used southern Angola to prepare its forces to liberate Namibia.

The response of the South African government was threefold. First, Vorster and P. W. Botha, who succeeded him in 1978, told the world that they wished to live at peace with their neighbours, whatever their colour. Second, they greatly strengthened the South African Defence Force (SADF) and let it raid across the border with increasing frequency (see Source 2). Third, they tried to weaken their neighbours by giving secret support to their rivals and by encouraging civil war.

Angola and Mozambique

In Angola, South African forces supported first the FNLA and then UNITA. They secretly raided deep into Angola and were often victorious. However, both in 1975 and, more seriously, in 1978, they came up against well-armed Cuban troops with air and missile support and had to retreat. Nonetheless, by

Source 4

South African troops of the SADF withdraw from Angola after a raid deep into the country in 1976.

backing UNITA against the Angolan (MPLA) government in Luanda, they helped to keep going a destructive civil war, which left the Angolan government very weak.

In Mozambique they followed a similar policy. Machel soon showed that he would never be a friend of a white-run state so the South African government provided money and weapons to a rival party, RENAMO, which spread a civil war across much of northern Mozambique.

Rhodesia

As far as Rhodesia was concerned, Vorster in 1974 decided that Ian Smith's white government had little chance of survival. He withdrew the South African police who had been helping the Rhodesian forces against the black nationalist guerrillas and encouraged Smith to share power with moderate blacks. Eventually Smith agreed to a general election in 1980. Both he and the South African government believed that the moderate blacks would win and set up a new government that was reasonably friendly to South Africa. But the strongly nationalist and anti-South African Robert Mugabe and his ZANU Party won an overwhelming majority.

Questions

1. Study Sources 1 and 2 and re-read pages 78–81.
   Draw a sketch-map of southern Africa, showing South Africa, Angola, Botswana, Malawi, Mozambique, Namibia, Zambia and Zimbabwe.
2. Write brief notes next to the following countries, describing the changes that took place there in 1974–75: Angola, Mozambique, Zimbabwe.
3. In a different colour, write brief notes next to South Africa, describing the responses of the South African government to those changes.
4. Finally, write a few sentences explaining how events started to weaken white rule in South Africa.

New forms of black resistance

Black resistance took on two different but effective forms in the 1970s: industrial action and the Black Consciousness movement. The white government found both difficult to handle and, eventually, decided that it needed to think about reforms. In the meantime its security police murdered some of the black leaders and detained many more.

Why and with what results did blacks change their methods of resistance?

The successes of the security police between 1961 and 1963 weakened black resistance for the rest of the 1960s. The main black leaders had either been imprisoned on Robben Island or forced into exile, the ANC and PAC were banned and the government was both swift and harsh in its use of all its repressive laws. The 1970s however were very different.

Industrial unrest, 1973

In the 1960s, the average number of blacks taking strike action was tiny – about 2,000 each year. In 1973 it rocketed upwards, with 160 strikes involving 61,000 workers in the first three months alone. The main centres of action were Durban and the East Rand; the main causes, wages not keeping pace with rising prices, and bad management. These strikes were difficult for the companies and government to defeat because the strikers had short, sharp, mass walk-outs and avoided electing leaders whom the companies and government could pick on. In contrast to earlier strikes, they steered clear of political campaigning. The strikes were successful, not just in winning better wages but also in breathing life into the trade-union movement. White employers worried more about the future, should apartheid fail to change.

Black Consciousness

Ever since organised black resistance movements had begun in the nineteenth century, the question of how far blacks should allow whites into these movements had been an important and difficult one. Within the ANC Youth League in the 1940s, Anton Lembede had stressed that 'Africa was a black man's country' and that the ANC must above all be a black nationalist movement. The ANC, however, preferred a more multi-racial approach, which the Freedom Charter of 1955 sets out clearly. Robert Sobukwe and the PAC also insisted that blacks must liberate themselves, a view which the Black Consciousness movement of the 1970s held even more strongly.

Black Consciousness started as a university student movement. A number of black students, the most influential of whom was Steve Biko, decided that the National Union of South African Students (NUSAS), which was white-dominated, could not properly look after black students, even though it was strongly critical of apartheid. In 1969 they formed

Source 1

Relaxing at the Zanempilo clinic. From left to right: Steve Biko, Dr Mamphela Ramphele and Mxolisi Mvovo, Steve's brother-in-law.

SASO, the South African Students Organisation, with Biko as its first president.

Steve Biko

Steve Biko was born in 1946, in a poor family in King William's Town in the Eastern Cape. His father died when he was young and his mother somehow made sure that he got a decent education. He attended the non-white section of the Natal University medical school and was active in NUSAS before leading the SASO breakaway. Biko was a powerful writer and thinker, an eloquent speaker and also a man of much charm and many friends.

In SASO newsletters in articles headed 'I write what I like' and signed 'Frank Talk', he explained his ideas of Black Consciousness. He argued that as a result of living for generations in a white-dominated society, black people had lost confidence in themselves. They came to assume that the whites were superior so they accepted too easily, if unhappily, the bad ways in which they were treated.

Source 2

Steve Biko, 'We Blacks', an article in his book *I Write What I Like*, 1988.

In the privacy of his toilet, [the black man's] face twists in silent condemnation of white society, but brightens up in sheepish obedience as he comes out in response to his master's impatient call.

Acting as a witness in defence of some of his SASO friends who were on trial, he told this story about a white man he knew, who was installing electricity with a black assistant:

Source 3

Steve Biko, *I Write What I Like*, 1988.

[The white man] had to be above the ceiling and the black man was under the ceiling and they were working together pushing up wires ... all the time there was insult, insult, insult from the white man.... I ask him: why do you speak like this to this man? and he says to me in front of this guy: it's the only language he understands, he is a lazy bugger. And the black man smiled. I asked him if it is true and he says: no, I am used to it.

[Later, when the black man was on his own, Biko asked him how he really felt.] The man changed, he became very bitter, and he was telling how he wants to leave at any moment, but what can he do? ... he has got to work, he has got to take it.

Until they had confidence in themselves and their society, Biko said, blacks would never gain their freedom, and to regain their confidence they must end their dependence on the whites. With friends he set up the Black Community Programmes in which blacks helped other blacks without white assistance. The most successful of these was the Zanempilo Community Health Clinic, near King William's Town, run by Dr Mamphela Ramphele, whom Biko had met at medical school (see Source 1).

The murder of Steve Biko

Biko's reputation grew both in South Africa and internationally. The ideas of Black Consciousness caught on particularly among young blacks. The government banned him in 1973 and then detained him without trial for a few months in 1976. In 1977 they had him arrested again. The Port Elizabeth police kept him naked in a cell for eighteen days. A five-man interrogation team beat him up so badly that he went into a coma. 'There was a scuffle,' said the officer in charge. 'Mr Biko hit his head against a wall.' He was then driven, unconscious and naked under a blanket in the back of a Land Rover 1,000 kilometres for treatment in a Pretoria hospital. There he died, aged 30. A close colleague on the community project work, Mapetla Mohapi, had already been murdered in detention. The police story was that he had hanged himself, using his jeans. Dr Ramphele was banished to northern Transvaal, her clinic and all the other projects closed down and most of the other Black Consciousness leaders banned or detained.

Biko's death leaves police chief 'cold'

Source 4

The *Guardian* reports Biko's death and the comment of Kruger, the Nationalist minister responsible for the police, September 1977.

Such cruelty and destructiveness backfired. One effect of Black Consciousness was to make young people ready to defy the government and police at almost any cost. Biko's murder just added fuel to a fire which the white government never fully succeeded in putting out.

Questions

Study sources 1–3.

1 **a** Explain in your own words what Steve Biko meant by 'Black Consciousness'.
b How did the Black Consciousness movement differ from previous forms of black resistance?

2 Read Source 3. According to Steve Biko, why did the black man not say how he really felt while the white man was present?

3 **a** Read pages 83–84. Find four actions taken by Steve Biko in his Black Consciousness campaign.
b How do these actions help to explain why the police treated Steve Biko so brutally?

The Soweto riots 1976

Soweto is a huge collection of townships to the south-west of Johannesburg. In June 1976, the schoolchildren of Soweto began rioting against government education policies. The riots lasted for months and spread all over the country. Though the army and police eventually ended the riots, they did so at great cost in human suffering. The uneasy calm which followed did not last long.

Source 1

The marches which began the riots. Thousands of young people fill the Soweto streets, June 1976.

How did the Soweto troubles of 1976 differ from those of Sharpeville and Langa in 1960?

Causes of the riots

The rioting began when 15,000 pupils took to the streets to protest against a new government ruling that half their lessons should be taught in Afrikaans (see Source 2). For them, Afrikaans was the language of their oppressors. Since no one in the world spoke Afrikaans except the Afrikaners, it was far less useful than English. The 'more Afrikaans' ruling seemed yet more proof that the white government intended black education to do nothing more than prepare them to be servants or unskilled workers. And yet they had to pay for their schooling in overcrowded classes with poorly qualified teachers, while white children had free education, decent buildings, smaller classes and qualified staff.

Source 2

'To hell with Afrikaans! What use is it to us?' the pupils asked.

There were other reasons for the rioting. Black unemployment was rising. The Transkei Bantustan was about to become fully 'independent', so many blacks working in the cities feared that they would soon be forcibly moved to that already overcrowded 'homeland'. In Soweto itself, houses were scarce because the government had slowed down the building programme there in order to speed it up in the Bantustans.

Another recent act by the government had angered urban blacks. It had abolished the urban local authorities and replaced them with local boards. By this change, the costs of running the townships, including the salaries of the white officials of the new boards, passed from white local authorities like the Johannesburg City Council, to the black residents, most of whom could ill afford the extra charges. Dr Edelstein, a social researcher and one of the two whites to die on the first day of rioting, had already warned that anger was boiling up dangerously in Soweto.

The protest march

As the marchers made their way through the townships, more and more children joined them. But before they could go further, police stood across the road and blocked their way. The writer Mbulelo Mzame told the story of that day in the form of a short novel, *Children of Soweto*, which he based on eye-witness reports. In Source 3 he describes what happened when the marchers were halted by the police.

Source 3

M. V. Mzame, *Children of Soweto*, 1982.

> The police, addressing us first in Afrikaans and then in broken Zulu tried to order us to disperse. But we had grievances which could no longer wait. We surged forward, aiming to sweep them out of our path if they would not give way. By now our frenzied numbers had swelled and swelled. We shouted 'Amandla' (Power). 'Inkululeko ngoku' (Freedom in our lifetime) and 'One Azania*, One Nation' as we marched on, our clenched fists held high.

* **Azania** The name the Black Consciousness movement preferred to South Africa.

When the marchers refused to disperse, despite warning shots and tear gas, the police fired into the crowd, killing two youngsters and wounding several more. Source 4 shows the first of their victims.

The riots begin

The news of these deaths caused first Soweto and then other townships to erupt into demonstrations, riots and destructive violence which were to last for months and, in some places, especially the schools, for years. Most of the violence was directed against government buildings and blacks working for the government.

The main organiser of the Soweto disturbances was the Students' Representative Council. It led marches, persuaded workers to take part in one-day political strikes, attacked bottle stores and beer halls (since it believed with some reason that heavy drinking by some of the older people was weakening their will to resist the whites), and campaigned against rent rises.

Source 4

Hector Pietersen, the first victim of the riot police, 16 June 1976.

The riots spread

The Sowetan troubles spread swiftly to the rest of the country. The library and administration block of the University of Zululand were burnt down on 18 June 1976, the Assembly Building in Bophuthatswana in August. The centre of Cape Town saw serious rioting in August and September. Schools stayed closed for most of the rest of 1976 and the annual school examinations had to be postponed.

Results of the riots

The police met violence with violence. Nearly 6,000 people were arrested between June 1976 and February 1977. As many as 14,000 school pupils and university students fled the country, many joining the ANC in exile. Hundreds of pupils were caned for demonstrating, an 8-year-old getting five strokes for being present at 'an illegal gathering'.

The destruction was great, nearly all of it in black areas: 350 schools, 250 bottle stores and beer halls, 170 shops, many clinics, banks, libraries, post offices and 200 private homes. More than 700 blacks died. The police killed many of them. Others died at the hands of blacks who believed them to be police informers or to have helped the white government in other ways. Older migrant hostel workers, encouraged by the police, turned against the rioters and killed some. Near Cape Town, a young wife had to watch this.

Source 5

Quoted in Denis Herbstein, *White Man We Want to Talk to You*, 1978.

There was a knock on the door. My husband opened the door and saw the riot police who then allowed a group of migrants to come in, and they beat my husband until he was half-dead. One riot policeman remarked, 'You are lucky he is not stone dead.' Minutes later my husband died of head injuries.

The government told the world that there was no crisis and blamed the riots on over-excited young people stirred up by trouble-makers like the

Communists, ANC and Black Consciousness. It set up a Commission of Inquiry headed by Mr Justice Cillie who blamed the riots on officials being badly informed about the discontent in Soweto. That this discontent turned into a revolt was due to 'agitators' who 'intimidated' (frightened) people into rioting. So he concluded, incredibly, there was nothing really political about these riots:

Source 6

Quoted by Tom Lodge in *Black politics in South Africa since 1945*, 1983.

* **dispensation** Situation.

> Because of this intimidation ... it cannot be said that the riots were an expression of the Black man's wish or that, by rioting, he was raising his voice against oppression and for a more democratic dispensation* in the Republic of South Africa.

However, whatever they might say in public, Nationalist politicians knew that their world had changed. Soweto let loose by far the largest period of unrest in South Africa's history. After Sharpeville in 1960, the police were quickly back in complete control. After Soweto they could never be sure of the townships, which became increasingly ready to shelter ANC guerrillas. Soweto also shook white business, which began to put pressure on the government for reform. The riots also provided vivid television pictures which were flashed round the world and turned international opinion even more against white South Africa.

The effect of black resistance on white opinion

In 1977 Vorster called a general election. The message of the riots for most whites was the need for a tough government, and they voted heavily for the Nationalists. They won their greatest ever victory, taking 134 seats, their greatest number ever. The opposition parties took only 30.

Questions

1. Study pages 85–87.
   a What do Sources 1 and 2 suggest was the main reason for the pupils' march?
   b What further reasons can be found in Source 3?
   c Why do you think that the police opened fire?
2. Source 4 has become one of the best-known pictures from South Africa in the 1970s. Why do you think this should be so?
3. Re-read pages 88–89. What effect did these terrible events have on:
   a black opinion;
   b white opinion;
   c world opinion?
4. When Steve Biko was asked just before he died what evidence he had that Black Consciousness had influence in South Africa, he answered in one word – 'Soweto'. Judging by what you have read on pages 86–87, what connections were there between the Black Consciousness movement and the riots in Soweto?

Unit 6 Review

Questions

1 According to Verwoerd's Grand Apartheid design, by 1978 the world should have seen the following developments in South Africa:

- race relations in South Africa should be improving;
- the Bantustans should be gaining their independence and blacks be flooding home to them out of the white cities, where for the first time the proportion of whites to blacks should be rising in the whites' favour;
- South Africa's neighbours should be appreciating South Africa's success and wishing to cooperate closely with it, especially in economic matters;
- the world would have realised how sensible 'separate development' was and be happy to have South Africa back in the international community.

Using the information in Unit 6, explain why each of those developments did not take place as Verwoerd intended.

2 The Soweto riots were heavily covered by local and international TV crews. Prepare two programmes, one as if made by the South African Broadcasting Company (SABC) which was strictly controlled by the government, and the second by the BBC's 'Panorama' team. The programmes are intended to make clear what actually happened in Soweto in June 1976 and its causes. How will the two programmes differ? In your answer you should try to explain:

- the bits of film that each production team will be looking for;
- the kind of people to be interviewed to discover the causes;
- the background information to include.

Unit 7 · Sliding towards disaster, 1977–89

The crisis years of 1973–77 made the Nationalists realise that they needed to change their policies. They decided, on the one hand, to be even tougher on their enemies and, on the other, to introduce some internal reforms, their aim being to win more support from the black middle classes. These proved ill-judged decisions which, in the mid-1980s, brought the country close to civil war.

'Total onslaught, total strategy'

P. W. Botha was leader of the Nationalists from 1978 to 1989. He believed that white South Africa was the target of massive external and internal attacks ('total onslaught'), which had to be met by an equally massive counter-attack led by the government and the security forces. They had both to outfight the enemy and to win the hearts and minds of the blacks ('total strategy'). This meant giving much greater powers to the security forces but also introducing some reforms.

Did the 'total strategy' change South Africa?

Botha was a hard-headed, aggressive man, famous for his hot temper. He came to power in unusual circumstances. Vorster, his predecessor, and Connie Mulder, Vorster's expected successor, had both had to resign because of a financial scandal. Previously Botha had been Minister of Defence and, as Prime Minister, he greatly increased the influence of the security chiefs within the government. General Malan, former head of the SADF, became Minister of Defence.

Total onslaught

A French military writer, General André Beaufré, who had fought with the French armies in their unsuccessful wars against nationalist guerrillas in Algeria and Vietnam, influenced Botha and Malan. From him came the idea of 'total onslaught, total strategy'.

In their opinion, the onslaught on South Africa was part of the communist drive for world domination. The Soviet Union and China were helping the ANC-in-exile and South Africa's black neighbours to overthrow the white government. Should the ANC succeed, a fully communist government of South Africa would quickly follow, as Source 1 suggests.

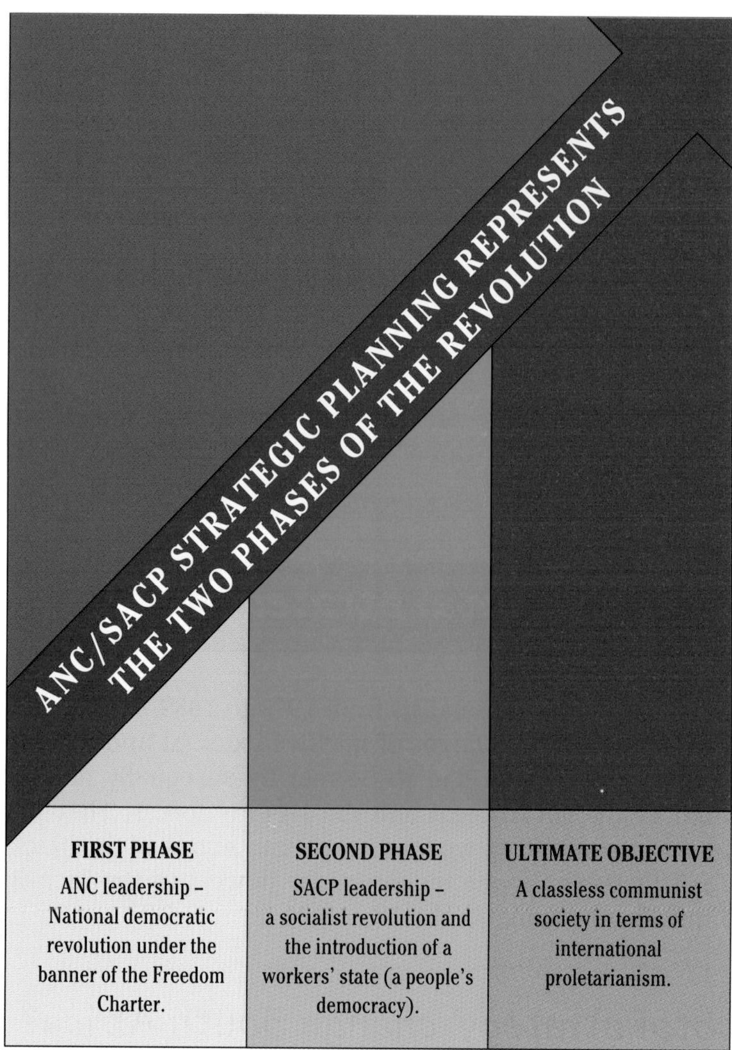

Source 1

The 'total onslaught' in the form of a diagram. According to Botha and his advisers, more power to the ANC must lead to a communist takeover. From the Bureau of Information's pamphlet, 'Talking with the ANC', 1986.

Total strategy: strengthening the armed forces

The first part of the 'total strategy' to meet this 'total onslaught' was to strengthen further the security forces. The highly influential State Security Council created a National Security Management System which divided the country into a network of security units in order to deal with resistance groups more speedily and effectively.

Spending on security soared. At the end of the 1970s, the regular army was about 17,000 strong, including 5,000 blacks. To this, white conscription for two years' military service added another 37,000. As well as conscription, all whites had to do another 720 days' training in the following twelve years and join the Citizen Force. In the mid-1980s, the Citizen Force numbered 130,000. Divided into local units, it was trained to deal with internal rebellions as well as attacks from across the borders.

Total strategy: destabilising South Africa's neighbours

The next part of the strategy was to give the 'front-line' states (the black states on their borders) the hardest of times if they gave any support to the ANC or were otherwise unfriendly to South Africa. As a senior security official put it:

Source 2

Quoted by A. Sparks, *The Mind of South Africa*, 1990.

> We want to show that we want peace in the region, we want to contribute.... But we also want to show that if we are refused we can destroy the whole of southern Africa.

The SADF raided wherever it believed there to be ANC guerrilla bases. Source 3 was one result.

The security forces also gave active support to UNITA in Angola and RENAMO in Mozambique, essentially keeping civil wars going in order to weaken their neighbours. The ordinary people of Angola and Mozambique were the main victims of this destabilisation policy. These violent measures had some temporary success. In 1984 Mozambique and South Africa signed the Nkomati Accord by which they promised to

Source 3
One result of an SADF raid on Mozambique, 1981.

interfere less in each other's affairs. Mozambique would not assist the ANC nor South Africa RENAMO. But this agreement did not last long.

Total strategy: reform

The other part of the 'total strategy' was internal reforms. Big business (see page 102) wanted apartheid changed so as to stay profitable. So too did the 'verligtes' (see page 70) within the Nationalist Party, partly to win more support from the better-off urban blacks and partly to improve South Africa's dreadful international image. The government therefore set up a number of commissions of enquiry which lead to reforms between 1979 and 1983.

In 1979 the government accepted the main recommendations of the Riekert and Wiehahn Commissions; Riekert reported on the situation of the urban blacks, Wiehahn on trade unions. Riekert reversed apartheid principles for those blacks with Section 10 rights by allowing them to buy their own homes and to move more freely in search of work. At the same time it kept strict controls to prevent other blacks from moving into the cities. The Wiehahn Commission recommended that trade unions should have more freedom.

Though the government did not accept the main recommendations of the De Lange Commission (1981) on education, it rapidly increased educational spending. Between 1980 and 1990 the number of blacks in secondary education trebled.

It also abolished some of the apartheid laws – the Mixed Marriages Act, for example. It relaxed the colour bar in employment and the pass laws, and allowed cinemas and theatres to play to mixed audiences. So Dr Piet Koornhof, Minister of Cooperation and Development, could tell an American audience in 1979:

Source 4

Quoted in W. Beinart, *Twentieth Century South Africa*, 1994.

> Apartheid as you came to know it is dead.

Constitutional changes, 1983–84

The most ambitious reform was to create a new parliament with three chambers, one for whites, one for Coloureds and one for Indians. A multi-racial Electoral College elected the State President (P. W. Botha was the first), who was also advised by a multi-racial President's Council. However, the new constitution made sure that political power remained firmly in white hands and had no place for the African majority. The Coloureds and Indians were not much impressed, less than 20 per cent bothering to vote in the first election.

Source 5

The new multi-racial Electoral College meets for the first time in the House of Assembly, 1984.

Questions

1 Re-read pages 91–94 and explain the phrase 'total onslaught, total strategy'.

2 Where does Source 1 (page 92) come from? What part of the supposed total onslaught does it show?

3 What part of the total strategy do Sources 2 and 3 (pages 92-3) show? How justified do you think that the South African government was in doing such things?

4 **a** Study Source 4, above. What do you think Koornhof had in mind when he made this speech?
b How 'dead' was apartheid in 1979?

The townships erupt, 1984–86

The government's attempts to win black support failed completely. On the contrary, the constitutional reforms of 1983, which did nothing at all for the black majority, were a match that lit an enormous fire of rioting. Between 1984 and 1986 parts of South Africa became ungovernable. Though the rioters never got close to overthrowing the government, the government could not fully restore law and order. The violence, often provoked by the security forces, was great. Much of it was black against black in the townships.

What caused the township unrest and what forms did it take?

P. W. Botha's 'total strategy' did nothing to lessen his government's unpopularity. In the eyes of urban blacks, for whom the reforms were mainly intended, they were too little too late. They appeared to be the actions of a government which had no intention of genuinely sharing power but was weakening. While the Riekert reforms gave them more security, in no way did it lessen their determination to get rid of white domination. The Wiehahn reforms boosted trade-union activity yet, instead of swinging the unions behind the government, the reforms led them to become more active in the resistance movement. Relaxing the pass laws meant that more unemployed blacks crowded into the townships, anxious, restless and angry. In many areas of township life, therefore, blacks were in a mood to challenge white rule.

Source 1

A crowded schoolroom.

Schools

Black schools remained centres of anti-government activity – if they stayed open, that is. Many pupils believed that, despite increased government spending on education, they were still getting a poor deal and refused to attend school at all. Sources 1 and 2 reflect some of the reasons why they felt like this. So, as in 1976, there were thousands of young people ready to take action, either in school or on the streets.

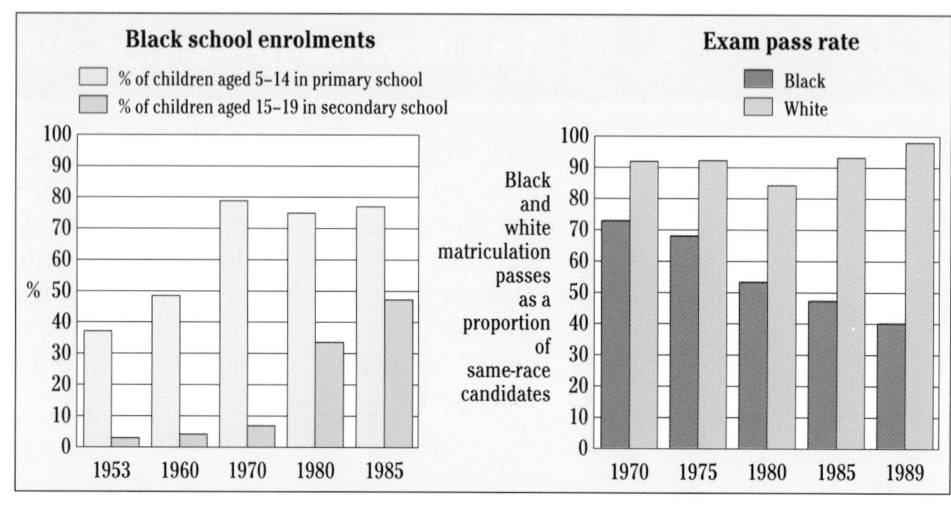

Source 2

Although the number of black pupils on school rolls rose considerably, black exam results got much worse, reflecting the pupils' poor attendance.

Trade unions

Black trade unions bargained toughly with employers and went on strike if need be. Where in 1974 only 14,167 working days had been lost through strikes, the equivalent figure for 1982 was 365,337. The black National Union of Mineworkers, led by Cyril Ramaphosa, organised major strikes in 1985 and 1987.

Source 3

One of the many strikes on the Rand. Goldminers outside the Chamber of Mines, Johannesburg 1987.

Growth of the black resistance groups

Black Consciousness (AZAPO)

The Azanian People's Organisation (AZAPO), the successor of Black Consciousness, stressed that blacks must free themselves from dependence on whites. It was anti-capitalist and looked forward to South Africa (Azania) becoming a black workers' revolutionary republic.

The ANC

The ANC continued to look forward to a future based on the Freedom Charter – a multi-racial, one-adult one-vote democracy, leaning towards socialism. Though still banned (see pages 44–45), it was gaining influence within the townships. Some of those who fled into exile after the Soweto riots of 1976 returned in secret to help organise resistance and begin guerrilla war. As in the 1960s, their main targets were buildings like oil refineries and power stations which could be damaged without loss of life (see Source 4). However, some guerrillas attacked buildings which housed people whom they thought to be supporters of the government, like the Air Force headquarters in Pretoria (1983) and the dockyards in Durban (1984). In both these cases their bombs killed innocent people, including blacks.

Buthelezi and Inkatha

Another important and active black group was Inkatha, which had started in the 1920s as a Zulu cultural organisation, but which Chief Mangosuthu Buthelezi turned into a well-organised political movement. Its aims were to end apartheid and strengthen the position of the Zulus in South Africa.

People found Buthelezi hard to assess. Since 1972 he had been Chief Minister of the government-made 'homeland' of KwaZulu, but had refused to accept Pretoria's offer of independence. He promised his loyalty

Source 4

ANC guerrillas blow up an oil refinery in 1980.

to Mandela, the imprisoned ANC leader, but he criticised the ANC for its guerrilla attacks and for its support for economic sanctions against South Africa. In Natal/KwaZulu he made Inkatha into a very large and strong organisation which was for Zulus only. Other black politicians disliked him because he was too ready to work with white business and too much the Zulu leader. Between 1985 and 1987 the differences between Inkatha and other black groups exploded into violence.

The United Democratic Front
The United Democratic Front (UDF) came into existence in 1983 to fight the new constitution. Its aim was to unite all the black resistance groups. Churchmen like Dr Allan Boesak and Archbishop Tutu were among its leaders; so too were ANC women like Albertina Sisulu and Winnie Mandela. The UDF grew at an enormous pace, reaching 2 million members in 1985. Like the ANC, the UDF was multi-racial and looked forward to a future based on the Freedom Charter. It stressed how urgent was the need to end apartheid forever:

Source 5

From a speech by Dr Boesak at a meeting in the Coloured town of Mitchell's Plain near Cape Town in 1983.

Let me remind you of three little words.... The first word is 'all'. We want all our rights, not just a few token handouts which the government sees fit to give.... And we want all of South Africa's people to have their rights. Not just a selected few, not just 'Coloured' or 'Indians'....

The second word is the word 'here'. We want all our rights here in a united, undivided South Africa. We do not want them in impoverished homelands, we do not want them in our separate little group areas....

The third word is the word 'now'. We want all our rights, we want them here, and we want them now. We have been waiting for so long, we have been struggling for so long. We have pleaded, cried, petitioned too long now. We have been jailed, exiled, killed for too long. Now is the time.

Violent protest, 1984–87

The biggest, longest and most violent uprising in South Africa's violent history began on the Rand in 1984. Rent rises sparked it off. Among the 1983 constitutional reforms had been the shifting of responsibility for black rents to black local councils. Very few blacks were prepared to stand as local councillors. Those who did were often corrupt and hated as collaborators with the Boers. In September, demonstrations against rent rises were met with police violence. Rioters then attacked black councillors, hacking them down on their doorsteps and burning their expensive houses and cars.

From the Rand, riots spread all over the country, in the countryside as well as the towns. Heavily armed riot police in their armoured vehicles (see Source 6) lumbered into the townships to be met by jogging, jeering, stone-throwing black 'comrades' who would scatter as they appeared and re-form as soon as they had gone.

The violence worsened in 1985. At Uitenhage in the Eastern Cape in March on the twenty-fifth anniversary of the Sharpeville massacre, there was another massacre. Riot police opened fire on a funeral crowd, killing twenty and wounding 27, mostly by shots in the back.

Source 6
An armoured personnel carrier blocks a street in 1985.

Source 7
'We will not be silenced'. A UDF poster of 1985.

The UDF kept protesting (see Source 7) and the riots worsened. In Natal/KwaZulu rivalry between the UDF and Inkatha led to the worst violence of all, which continued in the 1990s. The UDF suspected that the security police were secretly helping Inkatha. In time this suspicion turned out to be correct.

Black violence against blacks

Black groups also fought each other without any help from whites. In Soweto in 1985, supporters of the ANC were ready to fight supporters of AZAPO to a horrible death, though they all wished to overthrow apartheid. Rian Malan tells of the rivalry between the Wararas (ANC) and the Zim-zims (AZAPO) in 1985:

Source 8 Rian Malan, *My Traitor's Heart*, 1994.

> All that is certain is that Sipho Mngomezulu (AZAPO) was abducted and killed in broad daylight .... there was a second killing after his funeral. This time the victim was Martin Mohau, age twenty-nine. Martin was a hero of the struggle against apartheid.... He was also a Zim-zim. A mob of Wararas waylaid him on his way home from Sipho's funeral and necklaced him – put a car tyre around his neck, poured gasoline on him and burned him alive.

Government repression

In July 1985, the government declared a partial state of emergency which it extended further in June 1986 so that the whole country was effectively under martial law. It put strict control on the media so it was difficult to know how serious the unrest was. The security forces made greater use of vigilantes, 'kitskonstabels' (or 'instant constables', as they called them), mainly unemployed blacks whom they let loose on the 'comrades'. For nearly a month in 1986 such vigilante bands destroyed much of the Crossroads squatter camp near Cape Town, killing hundreds and making nearly 70,000 people homeless while the riot police stood by.

Source 9

Police move in on a protester, Cape Town 1985.

In some townships the police simply gave up trying to maintain law and order. Youth courts appeared which dealt out what they considered justice. They often regarded necklacing as a suitable punishment for their enemies.

Eventually, in 1986, after detaining about 34,000 people, including young children, the Nationalists managed to get the unrest under control. But nothing had been solved and P. W. Botha seemed to have no idea what to do next. More blacks now believed that liberation was round the corner.

Questions

Re-read pages 95–100.

1 Study Sources 1 and 2. What was the connection between educational problems and rioting in the townships?

2 **a** Divide a page into four columns. At the head of each column, write down the names of four black resistance groups that were active in the 1980s (see pages 97–98).
b In each column, write down the aims of the group.
c Highlight any aims which the groups had in common.
d In a different colour, highlight any differences between the groups.
e How do their differences help to explain why these groups sometimes fought each other?

3 **a** Study Source 5. What was the UDF?
b Why did it bring out the poster (Source 7) in 1985?

4 **a** What is a vigilante?
b Why did the security forces use them during the unrest of the 1980s?

White politics, 1978–87

President P. W. Botha faced difficult problems with his own party and with white business. He knew that reforms were needed. But he also knew that if he reformed too fast his party might split. Botha tried to keep his party united by acting toughly against the opposition and by talking frequently about the need for reform in the hope of keeping business and international opinion content. He succeeded in staying in power but failed to stop his party splitting in 1982, or to hold the confidence of local and international business leaders. Why could he not keep the National Party united?

Why did the National Party split?

The Herstigte National Party

Many Afrikaners believed that the pure apartheid of the Verwoerd years was the only solution to the country's racial problems and should not be altered. Already in 1968 three cabinet ministers had resigned when Vorster had allowed foreign countries to be represented by black ambassadors, and had formed the Herstigte (Restored) National Party. These followers of pure apartheid were known as 'verkramptes', meaning 'the narrow ones', in contrast to those who were ready to consider reforms, the 'verligtes', or 'enlightened ones'.

The Conservative Party

A more serious split took place in 1982. Led by Dr Treurnicht, eighteen MPs, critical of the new constitutional proposals – especially the idea of even limited power-sharing with Coloureds and Indians – left the National Party to found the Conservative Party (CP). During the crisis of 1984–86, the CP did well in by-elections.

The Afrikaner Resistance Movement

An even more extreme Afrikaner group was the Afrikaner Resistance Movement (AWB) formed in 1979. With its banners, uniforms, racism and obvious pleasure in breaking up meetings by violence, it had uncomfortable similarities to Hitler's Nazi movement.

The 1987 general election

In the general election of 1987, the National Party (NP) used its control of television to try to convince the electors that it alone could defend them against black revolutionaries and international communism. Source 1 on page 107 is an example of its propaganda. In contrast, the CP criticised Botha for rushing ahead with dangerous reforms.

At first sight, the results looked good for Botha. The NP won 122 seats (52 per cent), the CP only 22 (26 per cent). In fact the CP had done well, gaining the votes of 37 per cent of Afrikaners, who were worried by the fall in their standard of living and end of the colour bar. Ever since 1948, the National Party had held on to political power by keeping Afrikaners united behind it. The success of the CP was, therefore, a serious worry to Botha and caused him to act with even greater caution.

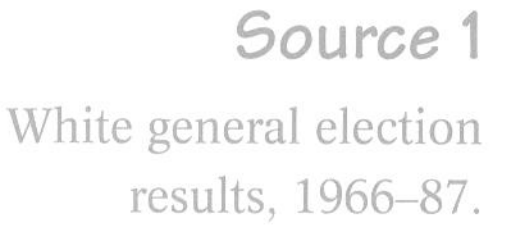

Source 1

White general election results, 1966–87.

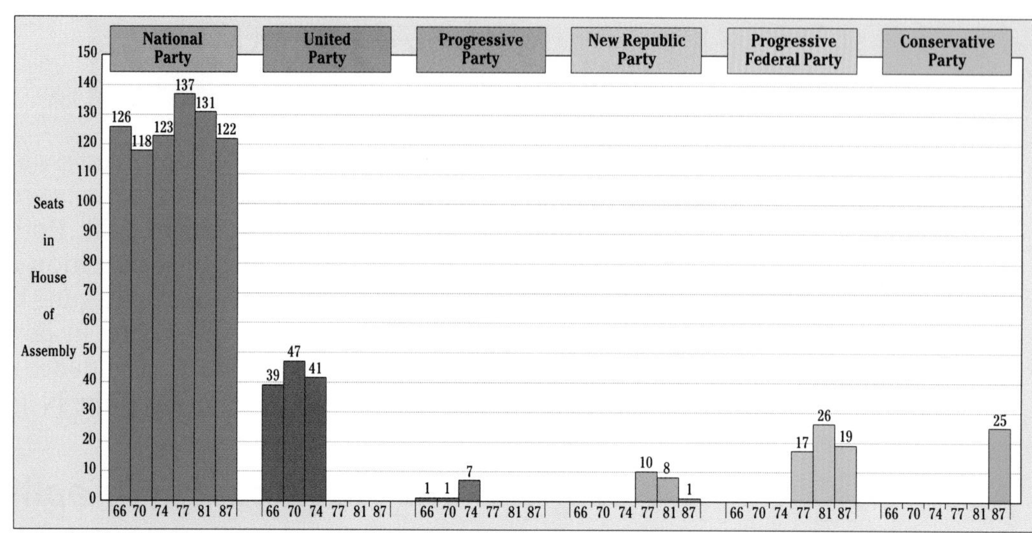

Economic sanctions

In the 1960s most Western companies had avoided criticising the Nationalists. They were making good profits under apartheid and, consequently, were ready to work with, not against, the government.

As we have seen, the 1970s saw a change of attitude. Business leaders found that apartheid laws were getting in the way of economic progress (see pages 68 and 82). They also found international criticism harder to live with. In 1973 the *Guardian* newspaper reported that only 3 of 100 British companies in South Africa were paying their black workers wages enough to keep them out of real poverty. It revealed that famous companies like Tate and Lyle (sugar) were paying particularly low wages.

Similar publicity in the United States roused Leon Sullivan to action. Sullivan was a black Baptist preacher on the board of General Motors, the world's largest car manufacturer, which had an assembly plant in South Africa. He persuaded General Motors and other US companies to agree to the 'Sullivan Principles'. In their South African factories, there would be equal pay for equal work, no segregation and better training for blacks.

However, many critics of apartheid argued that such principles were not enough. Western businesses should pull out of South Africa completely (disinvestment) and Western governments should impose economic sanctions. This would mean a ban on trading in goods vital to South Africa's needs. Only if the Nationalists suffered from such economic punishments would they give political rights to the blacks.

Sanctions: for and against

Reagan and Thatcher oppose sanctions

Botha was lucky in that Margaret Thatcher was Britain's Prime Minister from 1979 and Ronald Reagan the US President from 1980. Both were fierce believers in free trade and were strongly against any kind of sanctions. They were also convinced that white South Africa was an important ally in their fight against international communism, so they slowed down the international moves for sanctions against South Africa. In their opinion more international trade would mean better living standards for all South Africans and, eventually, political reform. He and Mrs Thatcher were also impressed by arguments such as the *Southern Africa Business News* headline below (Source 2). Sanctions would hurt the world, not just white South Africa.

Source 1

Mrs Thatcher, Britain's Prime Minister, with President Reagan in Washington, USA, 1988: united against communism and South African sanctions.

OCTOBER/NOVEMBER 1986

SOUTHERN AFRICA

Business News

Published by Africa International News and Features Vol. 1 No. 4

SOARING COAL PRICES WORLD WIDE PREDICTED IN FACE OF SANCTIONS

World coal prices are set to soar to more than $40 a ton if sanctions against South Africa are implemented by leading Western nations. The United States and Australia which are leading the campaign for the boycott of South African coal, uranium and steel products are high-cost suppliers.

South African steam coal is currently priced at about $26 a ton compared with the $40 a ton from the US.

South Africa is the third largest exporter of coal in the world after Australia.

In 1985 South Africa exported 44 million tons of coal mainly to the European Economic Community and Japan. More than 20 percent of Japan's coal comes from South Africa and an embargo would force the Japanese to buy the higher priced US or Australian coal which would probably escalate in price again without competition from South Africa.

Japan's Federation of Electric Power Companies says a South African coal import ban is unlikely to lead to a shortage of steam coal but it fears Australia in particular and other suppliers will take the opportunity to hike their prices.

South Africa's expulsion from the export market would have a major impact on many industries in the Western world. A one third increase in the price of coal would have a significant effect on numerous consumer products as well as domestic power costs in some countries.

Estimates of exploitable coal reserves in South Africa are 115.5 billion tons, of which 58.4 billion tons are considered economically recoverable.

It has been estimated that the exploitable reserves will last for at least another 400 years.

Between 1970 and 1981 the South African coal export trade grew from 1.2 million tons - one percent of the world's exports -to nearly 30 million tons, or 15 percent of world exports.

The huge Richards Bay coal terminal north of Durban has given South Africa the capacity to export annually up to 80 million tons of coal by the 1990's.

A survey by the South African Chamber of Mines Collieries committee, found that more than 35 000 coal workers are migrants from outside the borders of South Africa. Each black mine worker provides a living for an average of six dependants.

With a total of 95 000 blacks in the industry this represents 570 000 people dependent on continuing employment being provided in the coal industry.

Real average black wages increased by more than 300 percent in the period 1971-84 while average white real wages increased by slightly more than seven percent.

The government has also set the end of 1986 as a deadline for full participation in all job categories by blacks, thus eliminating the remnants of job discrimination in the industry.

It has given the reluctant white unions the deadline to agree on removing discrimination or have it imposed on the industry by legislation.

INSIDE THIS ISSUE

WATER a new era in communication.

HOUSING and $500,000 a day on new projects.

US CORPORATIONS spend big on social projects.

SOUTH WEST AFRICA resources threatened by fishing fleets.

Source 2

The front page of *Southern Africa Business News* in October 1986 argues that sanctions would hurt the whole world, not just South Africa.

The argument for sanctions

Reagan's critics believed that, without sanctions, mainly the whites would benefit and apartheid would last longer. As Oliver Tambo explained in a speech in 1986:

Source 3

Oliver Tambo, speech to the Royal Commonwealth Society in London, 23 June 1986.

The argument ... for sanctions is ... that such a massive blow would make it almost impossible for the apartheid regime [the Nationalist government] to stay in power.... The alternative ... is that we will be left with nothing but to fight it out with everything we have. The consequence of this is too ghastly to contemplate.

New demands for sanctions, 1985–86

The township unrest of 1984–85, which much of the world watched on its television screens, lent new strength to the sanctions campaign and weakened business confidence. Anti-apartheid shareholders gave their directors increasingly rough times at shareholders' meetings. International companies began to leave South Africa. For example, the British-based Barclays Bank sold its large South African bank network, partly because of a student boycott in Britain which had lasted many years.

Sir Timothy Bevan, Barclay's chairman, made the company's position clear in 1985 when he described apartheid as 'repugnant, wrong, unchristian and unworkable' and began talking with the ANC. So too did Gavin Relly, Chairman of 'Anglo' and one of the country's most respected business leaders. People in the United States and Europe refused to buy South African fruit and wine, and in 1986 the Common Market banned the purchase of South African iron and steel.

Source 4
British campaigners against Barclays Bank's investment in South Africa, 1976.

The 1985 financial crisis

In the summer of 1985 the township violence and international criticism led to more discussions inside and outside South Africa about the urgent need for greater reforms to apartheid. The world's press became convinced that Botha would announce such reforms at a speech in Durban on 15 August. When he came up with nothing except more tough talk, business leaders were particularly disappointed. The Chase Manhattan Bank of New York cut its links with South Africa and a major financial crisis followed. The value of the rand dropped by 35 per cent, the Johannesburg Stock Exchange had to be closed for four days and the government was forced to take emergency financial measures which increased black unemployment and hit white incomes.

The drawbacks of sanctions

Although world opinion swung slowly in favour of sanctions during the 1980s, there were still many people who firmly opposed them. Even among black South Africans, there was by no means total support for a ban on their country's trade. Source 5 shows some of the reservations that they expressed about sanctions.

Source 5

This article appeared in *The Sowetan* newspaper in March 1989.

SANCTIONS, VIOLENCE NOT RIGHT WAY - POLL

A MAJORITY of black South Africans oppose economic sanctions and violence as a means of ending apartheid, according to a poll conducted on behalf of the *Independent* and ITN, the television company.

Although a minority said that sanctions should be imposed on South Africa — even at the cost of their own jobs — the findings reveal that most blacks are unwilling to jeopardise job opportunities and financial well-being, and see the presence of foreign companies in the country as helping to sponsor change rather than support apartheid.

The survey, conducted by Markinor, an independent South African research company, of 550 South Africans living in all the main metropolitan areas showed that 54,7 percent were against the imposition of economic sanctions to bring about the abolition of apartheid.

Of the minority who supported sanctions, nearly three-quarters wanted them imposed even if it meant black job losses. However, a much smaller proportion of the total polled (only 8,8 percent) were in favour of sanctions if it cost them their own jobs.

According to the survey, not only do most black South Africans dismiss sanctions as a solution to the country's racial problems, they are also opposed to violence as a means of ending apartheid.

Over 61 percent said it was wrong to use violence. About one third of the more radical respondents (those who support sanctions even if it caused unemployment) believed violence was justified.

The survey shows that a majority of blacks believe South Africa's most pressing problems are economic rather than political.

Almost 58 percent said their biggest concern was either jobs, wages or unemployment. Only 13,5 percent mentioned petty apartheid regulations and a surprisingly small 1,6 percent the Group Areas Act which demarcates residential areas along racial lines.

A SURVEY by the London newspaper the *Independent* and ITN television network shows surprising resistance to sanctions by black South Africans. They oppose violence as a way to end apartheid.

They fear that sanctions could jeopardise jobs and undermine living standards, and see the presence of foreign companies as a hope of bringing change.

Regardless of attitudes to sanctions, nearly a third singled out unemployment as their key concern — partly a reflection of the fact that over 60 percent of those polled were unemployed.

The greatest concern about unemployment — 33.3 percent — was registered among those who supported sanctions

ARCHBISHPOP Tutu . . . pro-sanctions.

MARGARET Thatcher . . . anti-sanctions.

ment by foreign companies had little popular support. The vast majority — 77,9 percent — said that foreign firms should stay in South Africa and improve the conditions of their workers.

Only just over a third of those who supported sanctions even if it produces general unemployment said that foreign firms should sell their businesses and leave South Africa.

There was also considerable support — 37,3 percent — for the notion that foreign companies have a beneficial role to play in helping to end apartheid. Under a quarter saw foreign businesses as supporting apartheid

Questions

1 What are economic sanctions?

2 **a** Read page 103 and study Sources 1 and 2. What is the attitude of the *South African Business News* towards economic sanctions against South Africa?
b Which non-South African leaders agreed with them? Explain their thinking.

3 Study Source 3. Summarise Oliver Tambo's argument and explain why, in the long run, he thought that sanctions would mean less not more suffering.

4 **a** According to Source 5, what did a majority of black South Africans think about sanctions?
b Are you surprised that they seem to agree with Margaret Thatcher rather than Oliver Tambo? Explain your answer.

Unit 7 Review

For the 1987 whites-only general election the National Party produced a poster in the form of a letter to the PFP, the main white opposition.

A National Party poster for the general election of 1987.

Dear PFP leadership,

We're three days away from the election and you still haven't grasped what it is about.

We'll try one more time. So please listen carefully to some real experts:

> **"Our aim is to gain control of the two great treasure houses on which the West depends – the energy treasure house of the Persian Gulf and the mineral treasure house of Central and Southern Africa."** *Pres. Brezhnev of the Soviet Union (1973).*

Even you should know that in South Africa they're working at this through the ANC – 23 out of the 30 members of the ANC national executive committee are communists on Moscow's payroll.

Yet you want to unban them?

Here's another one:

> **"The struggle in South Africa is not between Blacks and Whites. It's between the supporters of genuine freedom and stability and those who wish to force a socialist dictatorship on South Africa with the help of international terrorism."** *Pres. P.W. Botha.*

It must be clear even to you, that the PFP's policy of publicly, consistently and bitterly opposing laws designed to neutralise revolutionaries before they do their evil work, of condemning and criticising the Police and SADF's efforts to prevent the ANC's 'people's war', is doing a great job for the ANC.

Finally, listen to another expert on how to take over a country:

> **"... when a country is demoralised, you can take it over without firing a shot."** *Lenin.*

The PFP's belief that you can talk the communists out of what they want, is naive to the point of being stupid. It's like saying the PFP can talk communists out of communism and their goal of world domination.

And by urging South Africans who truly desire peace to believe this, you're doing a great job of demoralising them. Because you simply create false hope.

Isn't it time the PFP leadership decided whose side it is on?

Because on 6 May the voters of South Africa are going to show whose side they're on.

They're going to vote for realism. They're going to vote NP.

Vote NP

It makes sense!

Questions

Study the first half of this poster carefully, especially the quotations from Presidents Brezhnev and Botha.

1 **a** Who was Brezhnev and why did the National Party quote him in the 1987 election?

b What did Botha mean by 'socialist dictatorship' and 'international terrorism'?

c Why would he not 'unban' the ANC?

d Use the poster to explain what Botha understood by the 'total onslaught' on South Africa.

2 How had he planned to defeat this onslaught?

3 How successful had he been by 1987?

Unit 8 · The triumph of the ANC

The ANC in exile, 1960–90

Verwoerd banned the ANC in 1960. Botha's successor, de Klerk, unbanned it in 1990. For many of those thirty years, its leaders in exile struggled to keep it in existence and its popularity in the early 1990s took many people by surprise. It owed much of its success to its President-in-exile Tambo and to Mandela, whose fame grew the longer he remained in prison.

How did the ANC survive during the years of banning?

Exile – being forced to leave your home and friends, not knowing when, if ever, you might return – can never be anything but a difficult experience. Nursing a badly wounded political movement back to health in exile must be an especially demanding task. This is what Oliver Tambo and a handful of ANC colleagues had to do in the 1960s.

Dali Tambo, Oliver's son who was barely two when he moved to England, recalls how, at boarding school, he was always worried that he would suddenly learn that his father had been assassinated, and how sometimes their car would clearly be being followed by people unknown and unfriendly. In their London flat, he said:

Source 1
Quoted by Hilda Bernstein, *The Rift*, 1994.

I knew there were guns around, I knew.... My father would be coming from Algeria, going to Lusaka, or somewhere like this and I'd see big suitcases full of money.... And I remember opening a suitcase up one time, and my father coming in – I thought it was toy money – and I said, 'Can I have some?' He said, 'No, no, that's for our people.'

The 1960s: getting established in exile

Oliver Tambo and his colleagues concentrated on two main activities. The first was to build up international support for the ANC in exile, not just in sympathy, but in money, in places to live and in arms for the liberation struggle. The second was to keep contact with the ANC within South Africa and, if possible, continue the armed struggle which MK had begun in 1961 (see page 45).

They had real success in their first task, getting both the United Nations and the Organisation of African Unity to treat them as the proper mouthpiece of South African people. Eventually the ANC had more official representatives in the world's capital cities than had white South Africa. Though groups like the Anti-Apartheid movement in Britain and the International Defence and Aid Fund supported it warmly, the governments of the United States and Britain were much cooler. The Netherlands and the Scandinavian countries helped with the living costs of exiled families but would not assist with funds which might be used for the armed struggle. The greatest assistance where money and weapons were concerned came instead from the Soviet Union and other communist countries.

An important base for the ANC was Tanzania. There the ANC leaders set up not only their political headquarters but also education and training centres for those young people who fled from South Africa. Other African and East European countries helped them to train their guerrilla troops.

Guerrilla attacks on South Africa before 1975 faced the huge obstacle of the white buffer states. Even to get to the South African border would have been an achievement in itself since the invaders had first to cross hundreds of miles of rough, enemy-controlled country. First in 1967, then in 1968 and finally in 1970 ANC guerrillas, linked to anti-Smith, black Zimbabwean guerrillas, slipped into Rhodesia, aiming for the South African border. On each occasion Rhodesian troops, supported by South African police, stopped them before they even reached the border.

The Morogoro Conference, 1969

In 1969, the ANC was in a bad way. Its guerrillas had fought bravely but got nowhere. Its exiles were depressed and divided. White South Africa flourished. Many exiles criticised the leadership for being out of touch and spending too much time travelling round the world talking to international leaders and not enough planning a revolution in South Africa. At a conference at Morogoro in Tanzania, all the previously elected leadership stood down. Some, including Tambo, were re-elected, some were not.

Source 2

Oliver Tambo, in the checked shirt, with African allies Presidents Kaunda of Zambia (left) and Nyerere of Tanzania (centre), 1975.

The conference decided that planning the rebuilding of the ANC in South Africa was its priority, though strengthening its international links was also important. It also agreed to widen its multi-racial appeal by allowing non-Africans to be active members of the organisation at all levels except at the very top, the national executive. The Indian Yusuf Dadoo and the white Joe Slovo both joined the revolutionary council which planned the liberation struggle.

The tide turns, 1973–77

The collapse of the Portuguese Empire, the weakening of white Rhodesia and the Soweto riots all improved the circumstances of the ANC. After 1974, it was able to set up guerrilla bases in Angola and Mozambique, close to the South African border. The Soweto riots led to thousands of able and politically active young blacks fleeing from South Africa. Many came to the ANC to continue both their education and the fight against apartheid. The training centre shown in Source 3 commemorates just one of the thousands who did so. It was named after a young man called Solomon Mahlangu who fled from Soweto in 1978 and joined the ANC. It trained him as a guerrilla and he was back in South Africa within a year. The group he was with killed some whites and were captured by the security police. He was tried for terrorism, found guilty and hanged.

The armed struggle in South Africa, 1980–85

After Soweto, MK was strong enough within South Africa to restart guerrilla attacks. While these were usually sabotage attacks on government or industrial buildings – a coal-to-oil refinery in 1980, a military base in 1981 – they also murdered police informers and blew up a shopping centre in Port Elizabeth, killing a number of civilians.

Source 3

A student at the Solomon Mahlangu Freedom College (SOMAFCO), so named in his memory.

The role of Oliver Tambo

What Oliver Tambo had to say was listened to with increasing care both inside and outside South Africa. It was a favourite ploy of the Nationalists to smear the ANC by saying that it was nothing but a puppet of the Communists (see page 92) so he frequently stated that the ANC was completely independent of communism. Certainly he worked with members of the South African Communist Party (SACP) because they too wished for the liberation of South Africa, but:

Source 4

Oliver Tambo, *Oliver Tambo Speaks*, 1987

* **detractors** Critics.

> Our organisations have been able to agree on fundamental strategies [basic plans] ..., whilst retaining our separate identities.... It is often claimed by our detractors* that the ANC's association with the South African Communist Party means that the ANC is being influenced by the SACP. That is not our experience. Our experience is that the two influence each other.

During the rioting of 1984–86 he called for an all-out effort to destroy apartheid. In a broadcast on Radio Freedom he declared:

Source 5

Oliver Tambo, *Oliver Tambo Speaks*, 1987.

> We have to make apartheid unworkable and our country ungovernable.

'I didn't think I was playing an important role,' he once said. 'I simply had a duty to perform.' In fact his achievement was enormous. In the words of Hilda Bernstein, historian of South Africa's exiles:

Source 6

Hilda Bernstein, *The Rift*, 1994.

* **disparate** Separate.

> For thirty years of exile he took the reality of apartheid all over the world. More than any other this quiet, gentle and friendly man held the disparate* forces and individuals in the ANC in a remarkable unity of activity and purpose.

Mandela in prison

Meanwhile, Tambo's closest friend, Nelson Mandela, though imprisoned for life on Robben Island, was strengthening the ANC too in an astonishing way. By the force of his personality, Mandela became the undisputed leader of the many political prisoners on the island. He insisted that, despite their loss of freedom, they should keep their dignity by demanding that their rights as prisoners should be fully respected and they should campaign for improvements at every opportunity. Michael Dingake, who was for fifteen years with Mandela on the island, recalled how:

Source 7

Michael Dingake, *My Fight against Apartheid*, 1987.

> Mandela made it a point to size up every Commanding Officer who was posted to the prison. As soon as the new CO arrived, he sought an interview with him ... he made it his duty to outline prisoners' grievances and acquaint the new CO with some of the unfinished programmes which were to the advantage of the prisoners.

Mandela also organised political discussions and encouraged other prisoners to study as he did for additional educational qualifications. To begin with, the prison regulations were harsh, but over the years they eased and a growing number of visitors came to meet the famous prisoner. None left other than impressed. The longer he stayed in prison, the more he became an international hero and symbol for human rights. 'Free Mandela' became a township rallying cry.

Source 8

Two old friends and campaigners, Mandela (on the left) and Sisulu, talking in the main prison courtyard on Robben Island in 1966. Their usual daily task was working in the lime quarry.

Questions

1 Re-read pages 44–48 in Unit 3 as well as pages 108–112.
a Why was the ANC banned?
b Where were (i) Tambo and (ii) Mandela in 1965?

2 What were the two main aims of the ANC during the 1960s? Why were the exiles so depressed in 1969?

3 What effect had the crisis years of 1974–76 on the fortunes of the ANC?

4 Explain how (a) Tambo and (b) Mandela had helped the ANC, though still banned, to be the most popular political movement for blacks in 1986.

De Klerk's new course, 1989–91

President P. W. Botha had a mild stroke in 1989. His policies were clearly failing and his relations with his ministers worsened. They forced him into a bitter resignation. F. W. de Klerk replaced him. F. W., as he was nicknamed, came from a famous Afrikaner political family. His father had been one of the architects of apartheid. F. W. was considered to be a conservative. He was expected to be at best a cautious reformer. His younger brother, Willem, who was much more of a liberal, wrote in a magazine article in 1989 that he did not expect his brother to do anything startling:

Source 1

Quoted by Allister Sparks, *Tomorrow is Another Country*, 1995.

> He is too strongly convinced that racial grouping is the only truth, way and life.

Source 2

F. W. de Klerk in 1992, campaigning successfully for his reform policies.

On the contrary, in his first big speech, de Klerk amazed his country and the world by setting his National Party on an entirely new course. Drastic changes were needed, he said, and announced the legalisation of the ANC, the PAC and the SACP and the release of hundreds of political prisoners, including Mandela and Sisulu. He went further, declaring his readiness to work with all political groups to create a new constitution which would give equal rights to every South African.

Why did de Klerk make such a drastic change?

Allister Sparks was a journalist present in the Cape Town Parliament when de Klerk made his crucial speech on 2 February 1990. He thinks that de Klerk did not fully realise what he was doing, and believed perhaps that through some clever power-sharing scheme the Nationalists might keep their hold on power.

Certainly, much of white South Africa underestimated the ANC. They may have been misled by events in Namibia (see Source 3). There the South African government had agreed that democratic elections could be held if the Cubans, who had inflicted serious losses on SADF raiding forces, were made to leave Angola. The Namibian general election was held in 1989, and though SWAPO, the black liberation movement, won, its victory was less clear-cut than expected. Simultaneously, communism was collapsing in the Soviet Union. These were signs, surely, the Nationalists hoped, that the ANC would weaken rather than strengthen.

Source 3

Sam Nujoma, the SWAPO leader, shakes the hand of one of his followers on hearing the news of a ceasefire with South Africa. SWAPO went on to win Namibia's first democratic general election.

Economic pressures

There were many other reasons, though, for de Klerk's change. The advice from his top economic advisers was that the country's economic position, grim now, would soon be far more grim if he did not abolish apartheid. The Broederbond (see page 23) was in favour of major change; so too were more and more Afrikaner politicians and businessmen who were meeting ANC leaders in English country houses and Swiss hotels and discovering that they were intelligent, respectable and reasonable. F. W. had trained as a lawyer and had a clear mind. He was a practical man, interested in what could work. He was also deeply religious, and his younger brother believes that he realised that with South Africa at the crossroads God had chosen him to lead his party in a new direction.

Nelson Mandela prepares for freedom

The Nationalists had been wanting Mandela out of prison for some years, just as long as he promised to give up politics. From their point of view, it would be much better if he lived out the rest of his life in quiet retirement rather than continuing to be the world-famous prisoner of apartheid. Mandela, however, refused to consider any deal which did not also include the release of the other ANC prisoners and their right to restart their political activities.

Though he remained a prisoner, the government moved Mandela from Robben Island to the mainland and began to talk to him informally about the future. It also instructed the prison commander to have him taken on car rides around Cape Town and along the coast, on one occasion leaving him alone in the car entirely unguarded! Mandela wrote in his autobiography:

Source 4

Nelson Mandela, *Long Walk to Freedom*, 1994.

> Much as I enjoyed these little adventures... I sensed that they [the authorities] wanted to acclimatise me to life in South Africa and ... get me so used to the pleasure of small freedoms that I might be willing to compromise in order to have complete freedom.

What the Nationalists were to discover in the next few years was that Mandela was a man of steely self-control who, despite nearing 70 and being in prison for more than twenty years, would do nothing for his personal advantage at the expense of the liberation struggle. In 1989 he met with both P. W. Botha and F. W. de Klerk, on both occasions saying that his freedom had to be linked with the unbanning of the ANC. De Klerk, he found, was a good listener.

Source 5

Nelson Mandela, *Long Walk to Freedom*, 1994.

> I was able to write to our people in Lusaka [Oliver Tambo and the ANC leadership] that Mr de Klerk seemed to represent a true departure from National Party politicians of the past ... [he] was a man we could do business with.

Source 6

Reunited after twenty-five years – Walter and Albertina Sisulu in 1989.

Source 7

Watched by millions of television viewers across the world, Mandela with his wife Winnie, leaves prison in 1990.

The ANC leaders are released

Walter Sisulu and other ANC leaders were released in October 1989; Mandela, his requirements met by de Klerk, in February 1990. The world's television reporters were at the prison gates in their hundreds and a huge crowd gathered in the centre of Cape Town to hear him speak in public for the first time in nearly thirty years. Despite the high emotions of the day, he gave a typically controlled performance, reading from a prepared text. He began:

Source 8

Nelson Mandela, *Long Walk to Freedom*, 1994.

> Friends, comrades, fellow South Africans. I greet you all in the name of peace, democracy and freedom! I stand here before you, not as a prophet but as a humble servant of you all, the people. Your tireless and heroic sacrifices have made it possible for me to be here today. I therefore place the remaining years of my life in your hands.

He then thanked all those involved in the liberation struggle, and declared that in no way would the ANC lessen its efforts to overthrow apartheid. To end the worries of the ANC in exile that he might be making his own deals with de Klerk, he pointed out that he was just one of many loyal and disciplined members of the ANC.

Mandela takes control of the ANC

The following month Mandela was in Lusaka, meeting the ANC national executive and convincing them that prison had not broken him nor clouded his judgement. He was elected Deputy President, and became the effective leader of the ANC since Tambo had had a serious stroke in 1989 from which he never properly recovered. In August the ANC formally ended its guerrilla war and most of the exiles returned to South Africa.

One of the last to return was Tambo, and the largest crowd seen at Jan Smuts Airport gave him a hero's welcome. His old friend Mandela picked him up by car from his plane and drove him round to the waiting crowd. Shaun Johnson, reporting for the *Argus* newspaper, described how:

Source 9

Shaun Johnson, *Strange Days Indeed*, 1994.

> He was lifted gingerly out by his aides, his frail legs placed on the ground. His gaunt face, with grizzled white beard, split into a grin of purest joy as he caught sight of the welcoming throngs.... They roared. He waved his left hand awkwardly, clenched his fist and grinned. It was a long moment of communion, without a word being spoken.

Questions

1 **a** Read pages 112–113. What changes did F. W. de Klerk announce in his first big speech?
b Why did people find this speech so surprising?
c What were the main reasons for this change of policy?

2 Mandela was still in prison in 1989 although the government had offered to release him as early as 1982. Why did he refuse to come out?

3 **a** What were the main points of Mandela's speech on the day of his release from prison (Source 8)?
b Why do you think he made these particular points in what was his first public speech for thirty years?
c What does this speech tell you about him as a political leader?

Civil war nears, 1991–93

At the end of 1991 the white government agreed to hold a Convention for a Democratic South Africa (CODESA) to work out with the ANC and other political parties a new constitution which would give democratic rights to all citizens. Both Mandela and de Klerk had great difficulties in keeping their supporters behind them and the CODESA discussions were slow and complicated. In 1992 the ANC walked out of CODESA. All the time horrible violence was flaring up all over the country and civil war seemed likely (see Sources 3 and 4).

Source 1
Mandela addresses CODESA, December 1991.

Why did the violence worsen after 1991?

CODESA

The CODESA talks were held in a large business exhibition hall near Jan Smuts Airport. Many political parties attended, but the two that really mattered were the ANC and the Nationalists.

The ANC leaders wanted a multi-racial, one-person-one-vote democracy as soon as possible. They were confident that in such a democracy they would be the ruling party. The Nationalists preferred a system which shared power between the racial groups and as far as possible safeguarded white rights. If a one-person-one-vote democracy had to come, then it should come slowly.

Mandela had many impatient supporters who wanted full democracy straight away, while many of de Klerk's Nationalists favoured delaying changes for as long as possible. In addition, Buthelezi and his Inkatha Freedom Movement wanted a special deal in Natal/KwaZulu and raised the violence against ANC supporters to new levels. Meanwhile, the AWB (Afrikaner Resistance Movement) threatened to assassinate Mandela and fight to the end for an Afrikaner homeland.

De Klerk held a whites-only referendum which, by a big majority, supported him in his negotiations at CODESA. In contrast, the ANC

Source 3

Inkatha attacks on a Soweto train, 1992.

Source 4

Deaths caused by political violence, 1985–93.

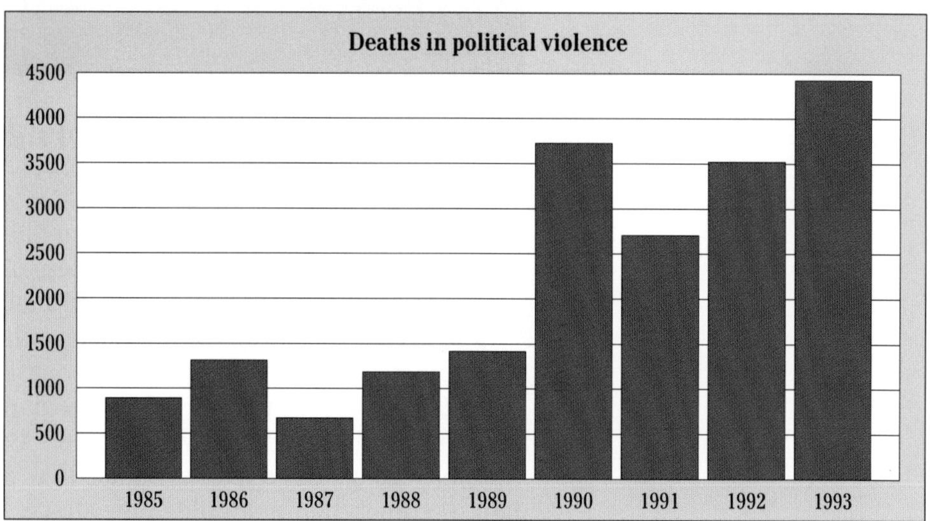

appeared more divided. The Nationalists slowed down the CODESA talks, hoping to weaken the ANC and strengthen their links with other parties. The ANC grew increasingly angry, believing that they were being misled and, worse, that the security forces, which were still white-controlled, were assisting Inkatha in their violence against the ANC. There were many rumours about a mysterious 'third force' spreading violence through the townships. In May 1992 the ANC pulled out of CODESA.

Zulu group linked to slaughter of 39

Source 5

How the Boipatong massacre was reported by the *Guardian* in the United Kingdom.

Boipatong

A month later, in Boipatong, a township south of Johannesburg, a group of Zulu migrant workers left their hostel during the night and shot or hacked to death thirty-eight people, including a pregnant woman and a nine-month-old baby. Residents were convinced that the attackers were Inkatha supporters and had been directed by white police. When de Klerk tried to pay a sympathy visit three days later he was driven away by an angry crowd, and in a confrontation between the crowd and the police, the police opened fire, killing another three people.

Source 6

Demonstrating for peace, Johannesburg, 1992.

Bisho

Boipatong caused the ANC to end all talks with de Klerk, who seemed to be unwilling or unable to make his security forces protect ANC followers. It organised strikes and demonstrations. One of these, in September 1992, was a march on Bisho, capital of the Ciskei Bantustan. The ANC planned to abolish all Bantustans. The Ciskei dictator, Oupa Gqozo, was very unpopular. The ANC hoped that its march would lead to Gqozo's resignation. In fact it led to the deaths of twenty-eight marchers and the wounding of 200 more. Gqozo's troops simply machine-gunned the unarmed demonstrators as they reached the Ciskei border.

Meanwhile, the continuing violence in Natal, where ANC Zulus fought Inkatha Zulus, some of whom were paid and trained in secret by members of the security forces, was taking hundreds of lives.

These were, wrote Mandela, the darkest hours before the dawn. Both he and de Klerk realised that time was running out if South Africa was to avoid a full-scale civil war. Mandela contacted de Klerk and they signed a Record of Understanding to reduce violence, and, most importantly, get the constitutional talks going again.

The constitutional agreement

At last, in November 1993, a deal was made. By their tough negotiating linked to their obvious readiness to give the whites a stake in the new South Africa, the ANC leaders got very much what they wanted. There would be a one-person-one-vote election on 27 April 1994. Four hundred MPs would be elected by a system of proportional representation. In order to give a sense of belonging to all parties in this important but difficult period of change, there would be a government of National Unity for five years. The President would be elected by the new MPs. Any party which won more than 80 seats would have a Deputy President, and any party with over 5 per cent of the national vote would have a position in the government. Nine new provinces would replace the old provinces and Bantustans.

The deal was finally completed in the early hours of a November morning. At the end, Roelf Meyer, the chief Nationalist negotiator, presented a birthday cake to Cyril Ramaphosa, who had led the ANC team. Both were tough politicians but had become good friends. At times of crisis, of which there were many, their mutual respect had helped them to keep going. Shaun Johnson wrote in the *Saturday Star* about their extraordinary achievement.

Source 7

Shaun Johnson, *Strange Days Indeed*, 1994.

Ramaphosa had to negotiate a settlement fair to his expectant, maltreated followers, without crippling his former enemies. Meyer had the loneliest task of all: he, representing those who had everything, had to give to their former enemies what was rightfully theirs, while guarding a fair future for his own constituency [people].

Pre-election violence

There were some alarming events for the country to survive before the election. A white right-wing gunman shot down the ANC's Chris Hani, hero of the young comrades of the townships, while he was buying his morning newspaper. It took all Mandela's authority to prevent major unrest. A crowd of AWB thugs smashed their way into the World Trade Centre, shouted abuse and vandalised part of it. A packed church service in a Cape Town suburb was interrupted by a grenade-throwing gang who killed twelve and wounded fifty-six.

Buthelezi of Inkatha refused for months to have anything to with the new constitutional deal. He said Inkatha would not take part in the election. Violence further increased in Natal/KwaZulu so the government had to declare a state of emergency. At the last moment, after repeated appeals from Mandela, Buthelezi agreed that Inkatha would stand in the April election.

The battle of Bop

Finally, in March 1994, the extreme right wing, desperate to show that it was a force to be reckoned with, decided to go to the aid of Lucas Mangope of Bophuthatswana, another Bantustan leader in trouble. Mangope was refusing to allow his people to vote in the April elections in the hope of somehow keeping control of 'Bop'. Consequently, 20,000 civil servants went on strike and law and order broke down. The AWB leapt into their trucks and motor-cars and roared off to Mmabatho, Bop's capital, armed with hunting rifles and pistols. Once they got there, they behaved with remarkable stupidity, taking pot shots at whatever group of blacks they found.

The actions of the AWB caused the Bop army to mutiny against Mangope and turn their weapons against the AWB gunmen, who left as hurriedly as they could. Some, however, failed and were shot by the Bop police (Source 8).

Source 8

Seen live on South African television, two wounded AWB supporters plead, in vain, for their lives in the battle of Bop, March 1994.

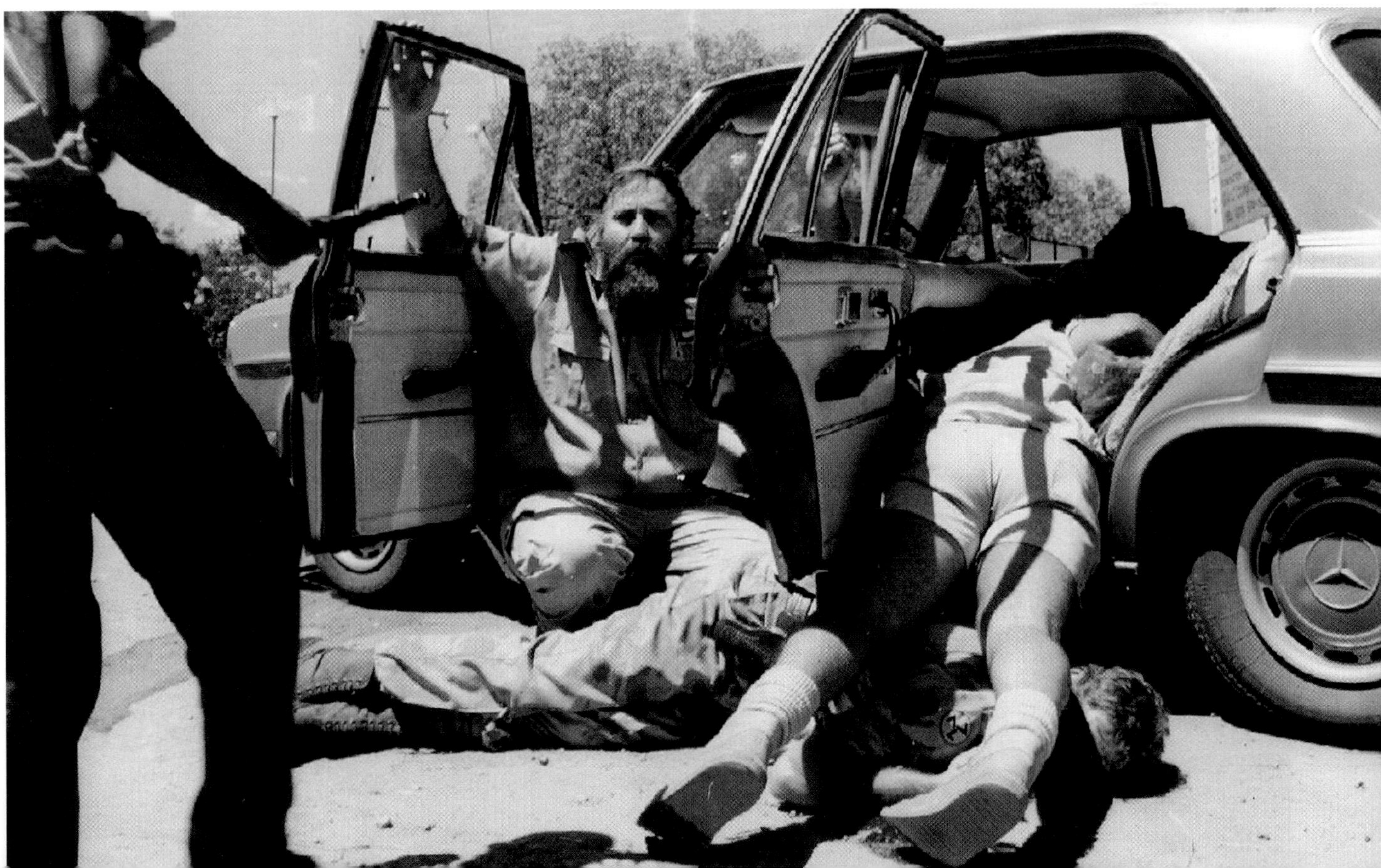

As well as providing dreadful television images of the end of white power, the battle of Bop also ended the threats of right-wing white violence to prevent the election taking place. White conservatives decided to take part in the election. As for Mangope, the government deposed him.

Questions

Re-read pages 117–121.

1 Why did the ANC stop talking to the Nationalists in 1992?

2 **a** What kind of violence did the country face in the summer of 1992?
b What effect did it have on Mandela and de Klerk?

3 **a** What were the main points in the constitutional deal agreed by Meyer and Ramaphosa (see page 120)?
b Why, in the opinion of Shaun Johnson (Source 7), was it such a great achievement?

The general election, 27 April 1994

In the run-up to the election, the ANC made much of Mandela's fitness to be the new nation's first president. It played down its fighting and rather socialist past and played up its plans for the future development of the country and its readiness to work with big business. The National Party made much of de Klerk's skill as a reformer and its years of experience in government. It campaigned hard for the Coloured and Indian vote.

Source 1

The ANC election campaign: crowds gather to hear Mandela, Spring 1994.

An ideal result?

Though white racists let off bombs right up to the election, the voting passed off peacefully. Millions waited in long, patient, cheerful queues to cast the first democratic votes of their lives.

The results were as follows: the ANC, 62.5 per cent; the NP, 20.5 per cent; Inkatha, 10.5 per cent. Of the nine provinces, the ANC won seven, the NP one – the Western Cape (where they secured many Coloured and Indian votes as well as white ones), and Inkatha took Natal/KwaZulu. It was a nearly ideal result from the point of view of making the main parties each feel that they had achieved something. The ANC had a clear victory and Mandela became President, but its majority was not big enough to change the constitution straight away. The NP vote allowed de Klerk to become Deputy President and the strong Inkatha showing gave Buthelezi a minister's post in the new government.

De Klerk conceded defeat graciously. He said how much he looked forward to working with Mandela in the new government of national unity, and described him as 'a man of destiny'.

Source 2

Shaun Johnson, *Strange Days Indeed*, 1994.

He has walked a long road and now stands on the top of the hill...the journey is never complete, and, as he contemplates the next hill, I hold out my hand to him in friendship and cooperation.

For his part, Mandela, on hearing of his victory, proclaimed to his supporters 'Free at last!' He congratulated the NP on its performance and said that the time for quarrelling was past. It was time to:

Source 3

Nelson Mandela, *Long Walk to Freedom*, 1994.

heal the wounds and build a new South Africa ... time to drink a toast ... to a small miracle.

Source 4

President Mandela celebrates his inauguration with his deputy presidents De Klerk (left) and Mbeki (right).

Certainly in terms of politics, Mandela's use of the phrase 'a small miracle' to describe the triumph of the ANC in 1994 was fair, but the problems he and his government faced were awesome. The historian Nigel Worden ended his *The Making of Modern South Africa* in 1994 as follows:

Source 5

Nigel Worden, *The Making of South Africa*, 1994.

> The legacy of apartheid still hangs heavily over the country in the late 1990s as it faces major problems of unemployment, urban migration and population growth. How far this will test the popularity of the new government and of the ANC remains to be tested.

Mandela was fully aware of the task ahead for the country and, in his inauguration speech on 10 May 1994, he looked both back and forward. To the great crowd beside the Union Buildings in Pretoria he said:

Source 6

Nelson Mandela, *Long Walk to Freedom*, 1994.

* **emancipation** Freedom.

> Today, all of us do by our presence here ... confer glory and hope to newborn liberty. Out of the experience of an extraordinary human disaster that lasted too long must be born a society of which all humanity will be proud.
>
> We have at last achieved our political emancipation*. We pledge ourselves to liberate all our people from the continuing bondage of poverty, deprivation, suffering, gender and other discrimination.
>
> Never, never and never again shall it be that this beautiful land will again experience the oppression of one by another.... The sun will never set on so glorious a human achievement.
>
> Let freedom reign. God bless Africa.

Questions

Re-read pages 122–124.

1 What was the result of the 1994 election?

2 Why, then and since, have many people described the result as 'ideal' for South Africa's needs in 1994?

3 Why did the ANC gain such a clear victory?

Unit 8 Review

Source 1

Prime Minister D. F. Malan during his victory speech after the 1948 general election.

> Today South Africa belongs to us once more.

Source 2

From President Mandela's inauguration speech in 1994.

* **covenant** Solemn promise.

> We enter into a covenant* that we shall build a society in which all South Africans, both black and white, will be able to walk tall, without any fear in their hearts, assured of their ... right to human dignity – a rainbow nation at peace with itself and the world.

Questions

1 **a** Who was D. F. Malan (Source 1)?
b About whom was he thinking when he spoke of 'us'?

2 What had happened to the Boers/Afrikaners in their history to make them so:
a anti-British;
b worried about the 'swart gevaar' (black danger)?

3 What does the Freedom Charter (see pages 34–35) have to say about racism and multi-racialism?

4 What does Mandela mean by 'a rainbow nation at peace with ... the world'?

5 Why do you think he went to so much trouble to reassure the whites after all the suffering they had inflicted on the blacks?

Unit 9 · From Mandela to Mbeki

The new government

As President, Mandela's main concern was 'reconciliation' – bringing together the previously hostile races of South Africa and creating a genuine 'rainbow' nation. He called his 1994 government a Government of National Unity (GNU). It had two Deputy Presidents, Mbeki (ANC) and de Klerk (National). Though the ANC had won a massive victory in the general election, of twenty-seven ministerial posts, the Nationalists had six and Inkatha three, with Mandela's old rival, Buthelezi, as Minister of Home Affairs.

The GNU survived until 1996. In many ways it did well, but de Klerk found his relationship with the new President increasingly difficult. Mandela was angered by de Klerk's refusal to tell the truth about his government's links with the 'third force' which had done so much harm in the early 1990s (see page 120). De Klerk and his Nationalist colleagues left the government and the New National Party (NPP), launched with new leaders in 1998, was seen to be more and more irrelevant in the new South Africa. The Democratic Party(DP) led by Tony Leon took over as the main opposition.

Source 1

South Africa's whites, especially the Afrikaners, are passionate about rugby football. In the final of the 1995 World Cup, which South Africa hosted, the South African 'Sprinkbok' team of fourteen whites and one black, won a thrilling victory over New Zealand. Mandela, dressed in the Springbok' colours, received a rapturous welcome from the mainly white crowd and was clearly as thrilled as anyone by the success of the South African team. Also shown is Francois Pienaar, the team captain.

How did Thabo Mbeki rise to the top of the ANC?

Mandela was seventy-six when he became President. From the start he delegated much of the day-by-day business of running the country to Thabo Mbeki.

Thabo Mbeki was born in 1942, in the Transkei. His father Govan was a journalist, committed to the overthrow of the apartheid system. Govan was one of the group arrested at Rivonia (see page 47) and was imprisoned, with Mandela, on Robben Island. Thabo joined the ANC Youth League in 1956 and helped to set up the African Students' Association. After a short time in prison, Thabo left South Africa in 1962. In exile, he dedicated his life to the ANC and became one of its leaders. Crucial to his advance was his friendship with Oliver Tambo, whose political secretary and speech-writer he became in 1975. By 1989, he was director of the ANC's international affairs department.

Thabo Mbeki played a leading part in the discussions which led to Mandela's release from prison in 1990. He was also heavily involved in the CODESA negotiations which made possible the 1994 election.

Mandela might well have preferred Cyril Ramaphosa as his deputy. However, after consultation, Mbeki emerged as the clear favourite. The main reasons for Mbeki's success were his intelligence, his achievements in exile, and his ability to avoid making enemies. He was remarkably skilful in getting different personalities to work together.

The Truth and Reconciliation Committee (1996–98)

Source 2

Anthony Sampson, Mandela, The Authorised Biography, 2000.

Mandela believed that, with the exception of Hitler's genocide of the Jews, 'there is no evil which has been so condemned by the world as apartheid.' The ANC had to find a way to forgive without forgetting.

Mandela's solution to 'forgiving without forgetting' was to set up in 1996 the Truth and Reconciliation Commission (TRC). Although amnesties (pardons) had been granted to most of the individuals involved in the violence of the apartheid years, Mandela was convinced that the truth had to be told and through that process, with the guilty admitting in public the dreadful wrongs they had done, genuine reconciliation would come. Chaired by Archbishop Tutu, the TRC heard many confessions of appalling crimes, mainly of torture and murder. Most came from the defenders of apartheid but some too from the ANC side.

Source 3

An ex-member of the SA Security Police demonstrates his torture technique to the TRC.

The TRC published its findings in 1998, though both the NNP and the ANC, to Mandela's anger, tried to get sections removed. Although the anguish caused to the friends and families of the victims of the crimes which the TRC revealed was great, there is little doubt that the TRC was a vital part of the reconcilation process. Justice might not have been done but a truer record of the realities of the struggle against apartheid was written. It became easier for South Africans to put the past behind them and look forward to the future.

Questions

Study Sources 2 and 3. Use the sources and your own knowledge to answer these questions.

1 Why did Mandela believe that South Africa needed a Truth and Reconcilation Commission?

2 Do you think most white South Africans would have agreed with Mandela?

3 Why do you think both the ANC and the NNP objected to the TRC's report?

The economy

Source 1

Unemployment rates by race, 1994–97.

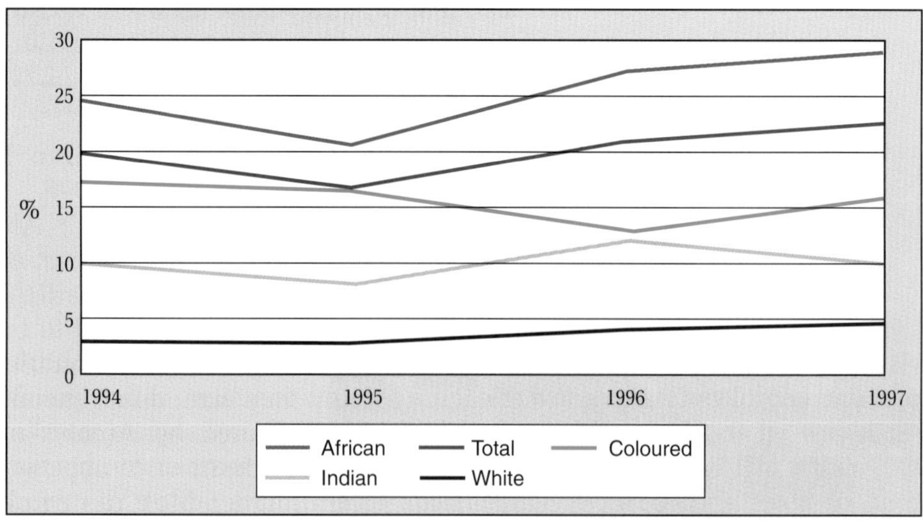

In many ways South Africa's most serious problem in 1994 was the high level of unemployment, particularly in the African townships where as many as one in four were out of work. As you can see from Source 1, the ANC government had no success in increasing employment between 1994 and 1997.

Before the 1994 election, the ANC had worked out an ambitious Reconstruction and Development Plan (RDP). Between 1994 and 1998 it aimed to build a million new houses, provide free education for all and considerably extend electricity and water supplies. Mandela hoped that the western capitalist world would invest generously in the new South Africa and set her on her feet, rather as US aid had helped Europe after the Second World War. To win the confidence of international business, he appointed white businessmen (Keys and Liebenberg) as his first two Ministers of Finance. However, the hoped-for investment did not come and international trading conditions proved hard for South African companies, with the gold price remaining comparatively low.

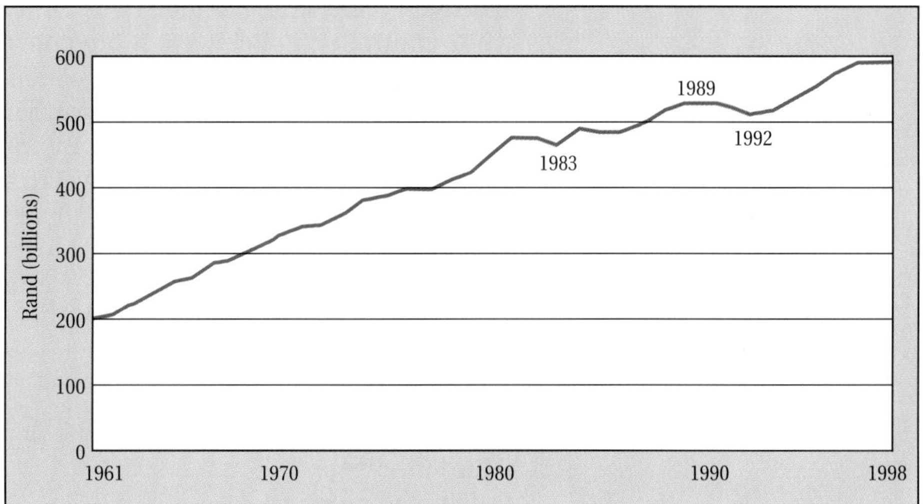

Source 2

Economic growth in South Africa between 1961 and 1998.

Although, as Source 2 shows, the economy grew between 2 per cent and 4 per cent between 1994 and 1997, this was not fast enough to have an impact on unemployment nor to pay for the RDP plans. Reluctantly, the government gave up its RDP hopes. Mbeki and Manuel, who had succeeded Liebenberg as Minister of Finance, replaced it with Growth, Employment and Redistribution (GEAR) in 1997. Growth, Employment and Redistribution aimed to encourage international investment by reducing the debts of the government through the strict control of government spending and by encouraging private rather than state-owned businesses. The aim was to achieve a growth rate of 6 per cent per annum, thus creating 500,000 new jobs by 2000.

There were many critics to GEAR both inside and outside the ANC. The most fierce was Cosatu, which represented the trade unions. Cosatu argued for greater public spending and against so great an encouragement of private enterprise.

Growth, Employment and Redistribution was not immediately successful, mainly because trading conditions remained difficult for countries like South Africa where mining is a major industry. In 1998, the growth rate was only 0.5 per cent and unemployment rose rather than fell.

Crime

Source 3

Anthony Sampson, Mandela, The Authorised Biography, 2000.

It was criminals rather than politicians who now appeared to pose the greatest threat to the peace of Mandela's South Africa. Gruesome headlines daily proclaimed murders, rapes, bank robberies and car-jacks, and Johannesburg was being described as the crime capital of the world, providing a growing deterrent to foreign investment.

South Africa had had a high crime rate for many years. The crime rate was fuelled by the massive unemployment which meant that there were hundreds of thousands of young people without work. During the apartheid years, crime tended to be concentrated in the African areas. The white-controlled police were more concerned with suppressing the black opposition than in reducing crime which affected white South Africa only on a small scale. With the end of apartheid, this crime spilled over into the white, business and tourist areas. By international standards it was very bad and the police force was not well trained to deal with it.

Mandela recognised that it was a very serious problem and, in 1997, appointed a leading business man, Meyer Kahn, to re-organise the police. As Source 4 shows, the number of crimes of some types had fallen by 1998, though others had increased.

Source 4

Crime trends in South Africa, 1994–98.

	1994	**1998**	**Increase (%)**
	Ratio per 100,000 of the population		
Murder	69.3	58.5	-15.6
Attempted murder	70.5	69.2	-1.8
Serious robbery	219.2	207.6	-5.3
Rape	109.6	115.8	+5.7
Assault	1043.1	1018.7	-2.5
Burglary	588.8	627.2	+6.5
Shoplifting	173.1	148.1	-14.4
Theft relating to motor vehicles	740.8	695.7	+6.1

Source 5

Anti-crime cartoon, taken from *The Sowetan*, 17th February 1999. Which mocks the governments failure to decide how tough to be on criminals.

AIDS

Another unforeseen problem which faced the new ANC government was the AIDS epidemic. This hit South Africa very hard, far harder than Europe or the USA. By the end of 1998 the Department of Health calculated that 3.6 million South Africans (nearly 10 per cent of the population) were HIV positive. The number was rising fast and included a much higher proportion of women than was the case in Europe and the USA. In the province of Kwazulu-Natal, 32 per cent of women attending ante-natal clinics were found to be HIV positive and the number of deaths that year outnumbered births for the first time since records began. The AIDS epidemic cast a long shadow over the country's future since it hit hardest young adults, economically the most productive generation.

The reaction of the government was confused and controversial. Mbeki agreed that there was a problem but, from 1997 to 2000, did not accept that it was as dangerous as it really was. He was attracted by the theories of a small number of doctors who argued that the link between HIV and AIDS was unproven and that South African AIDS was linked to poverty and hardship rather than to HIV. While he supported an anti-AIDS awareness programme, he was reluctant to give the go-ahead to the large-scale drugs programme which might stop or at least slow the growth in the number of AIDS victims.

Source 6

HIV-infection rates of women at ante-natal clinics. 1990-98.

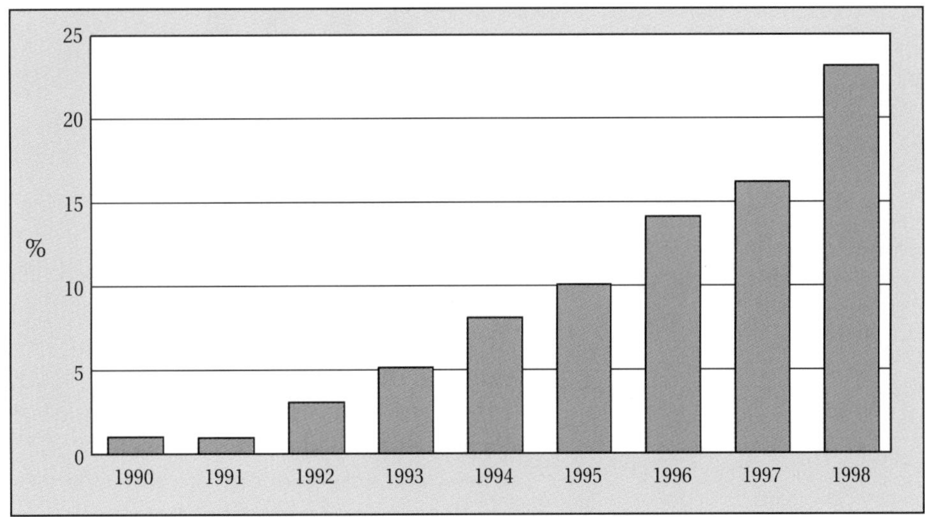

NEWS

Mbeki: The big debate

•THE QUESTION THAT CAUSED ALL THE TROUBLE:
At the first meeting of the AIDS advisory panel in May, President Thabo Mbeki asked scientists to explain how the disease had come to blight Africa.

He said AIDS had developed from one that infected predominantly homosexual men, intravenous drug users and haemophiliacs in the US and Western Europe in the '80s to one that affected a vast African heterosexual population less than a decade later.

"This is not an idle question for us because it bears directly on the question of how we should respond if this change is for reasons we cannot explain," he said.

•WHAT MOST SCIENTISTS SAY:
So-called orthodox scientists from bodies like the local Medical Research Council, the Centres for Disease Control in the US and organisations such as the World Health Organisation and UNAIDS say that AIDS is caused by the human immunodeficiency virus that is spread by unprotected sex, by sharing needles with an HIV-infected person and by infected pregnant women to their babies.

They say the evidence that HIV causes AIDS is overwhelming. First, evidence of HIV infection is easily found in patients with AIDS; second, the virus has been isolated and grown in pure culture from people with the disease; and, finally, studies of AIDS cases resulting from blood transfusions have documented the transmission of HIV to previously uninfected people who have subsequently developed the disease.

They say tests for HIV are reliable and that anti-retroviral drugs can be used to slow down the pace of infection and cut down transmission of the virus from mother to child.

•WHAT THE 'DISSIDENTS' SAY:
The so-called AIDS dissidents believe that HIV is not the cause of AIDS. They acknowledge that people are dying and that AIDS is caused by a breakdown of the immune system. But they say the disease has been caused in Europe and the US by recreational and anti-retroviral drugs and in the developing world by poverty, malnutrition and poor living standards.

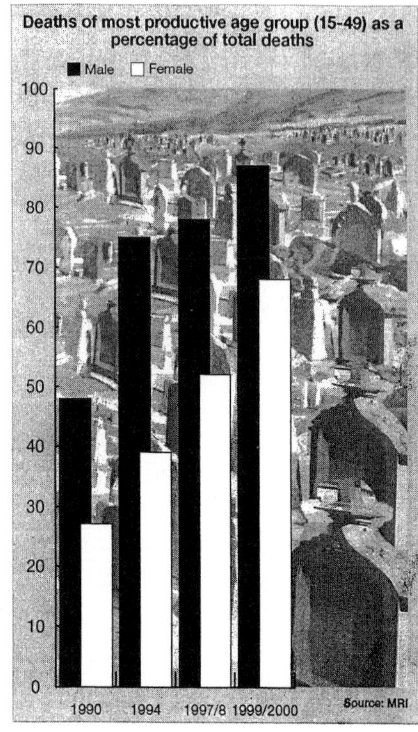

DYING YOUNG: The shocking graph above shows how the number of South Africans dying before they reach the age of 50 has almost doubled over the past 10 years — an increase attributed to the spread of AIDS.

AIDS

THE FACTS BEHIND THE SMOKESCREEN

As the International AIDS Conference begins in Durban this week, Laurice Taitz looks at what the deadly virus means for you

What it all means for SA

•South Africa cannot be compared to other industrialised countries because its epidemic is many times larger than that experienced by the worst-hit industrialised countries;

•In other industrialised countries the epidemic is largely under control and AIDS deaths have fallen significantly because of the availability of anti-retroviral therapy;

•In terms of percentages per race group, there are many more African people infected than other groups. But there is evidence that AIDS is spreading through all groups in South Africa and is breaching class barriers;

•AIDS is killing people in the economically active age group;

•In homes across the country, AIDS cases are causing untold trauma and are proving to be economically disastrous;

•Nearly one million SA children will lose their mothers to AIDS by 2005, according to the Department of Health.

Source 7

The South African Sunday Times, 9 July 2000.

Mandela's retirement

Mandela celebrated his eightieth birthday in July 1998 with his new wife, Graca Machel, the widow of the President of Mozambique. He had divorced his second wife Winnie in 1996 after she became involved in a number of personal and political scandals. In 1999 he retired, leaving Mbeki to fight the June election of that year. In his final speech to Parliament, he declared himself proud to be one of the generation 'for whom the achievement of democracy was the defining (most important) challenge' and to have helped South Africans to 'chose a profoundly legal (peaceful) path to their revolution'. Although his government had faced many difficulties and the deep and bitter social divisions which survived apartheid, he kept his country on the democratic path and through his commitment to reconciliation greatly lessened those divisions.

Tony Leon, one of his sharpest critics in recent years, described him as one of those exceptional leaders who like Gandhi of India:

Source 8

Tony Leon's tribute to Mandela on Mandela's retirement.

> ...was born with a special kind of grace who seem to transcend the politics of their age.

Leon's tribute explains why Mandela managed both to bring urgently needed and long-awaited revolution to his country peacefully and to lay the foundations for a secure democratic government.

The election of 1999

Source 9

The results of the 1999 election (the 1994 results are in brackets).

Party	Seats	% of vote
ANC	266 (252)	66.4 (62.7)
DP	38 (7)	9.6 (1.7)
IFP (Inkatha)	34 (43)	8.6 (10.5)
NNP	28 (82)	6.9 (20.4)
Others	34 (23)	8.5 (4.7)

Fewer voted in 1999 than in 1994 but the ANC increased its share of the poll. Inkatha's share fell slightly, that of the NNP greatly. The DP, in contrast, did very well in white areas and replaced the Nationalists as the main parliamentary opposition to the ANC.

Of the nine provinces, the ANC continued to govern seven. In 1994, Inkatha had had a clear majority in Kwazulu-Natal. This it lost in 1999 and had to share power with the ANC. In 1994 the NP won control of the Western Cape with a clear majority. This it lost in 1999 but the DP was ready to join it in a coalition to keep the ANC out.

Why did the ANC do so well?

The ANC won because, above all, South Africa remained a country where the political parties remained the parties of particular racial groups. The Africans are much the largest racial group and the ANC held on to the African vote. It held on to and increased this vote because most Africans thought that the ANC was doing a good job. Whites might complain about crime, AIDS, slow economic growth and fewer good jobs for their children. In contrast, most Africans saw a new African government effectively at work and benefits coming, if slowly, to their communities in the shape of electricity, piped water, new housing and health centres. They did not expect miracles overnight and the Mandela/Mbeki combination had done more than enough to keep their confidence.

Questions

Study Source 1.

1 What happened to (a) African, (b) Indian and (c) white unemployment between 1994 and 1997?

2 Why were these unemployment trends so serious for the ANC government?

Study Source 2.

3 How did the rate of national economic growth of the first ANC government between 1994 and 1997 compare with that of the last National Party government between 1989 and 1994?

4 To what extent did the 1994–97 rate of growth meet South Africa's needs?

5 In what way did the ANC government change its economic policy?

Study Source 4.

6 What do these figures tell you about trends in South Africa's crime rates in the 1990s?

7 How serious a problem was crime for the ANC government? What steps did it take to reduce it?

Unit 9 Review

Source 1

Nelson Mandela and Thabo Mbeki at the final pre-election rally in Johannesburg, 1999.

Source 2

Monitoring the 1999 election.

Questions

Study pages 132–133.

1 **a** What happened in the 1999 elections?
b Which parties did better and which worse?
c Account for the success of the most successful party.

Study pages 128–132.

2 **a** What were the main problems which the ANC government faced between 1994 and 1999? How successfully did it deal with them?

3 Nelson Mandela retired in 1999. He had been President of South Africa for five years. Would it have been better for his reputation if he had retired five years earlier?

4 **a** Describe the steps by which Thabo Mbeki became President of South Africa.
b What were his main qualities as a leader?
c What were the main problems his country faced in 2000?

Parties and organisations

ANC African National Congress – the oldest and largest black political movement in South Africa. Initially the SANNC (see below)

AWB Afrikaner Resistance Movement – extremist white group particularly active in the 1980s and early 1990s

AZAPO Azanian People's Organisation – black liberation movement in South Africa, which it preferred to call Azania, influenced by Black Consciousness ideas, particularly active in the 1980s

CODESA Convention for a Democratic South Africa – the lengthy multi-racial and multi-party meetings in 1992-3 which decided how democracy should start in South Africa

CPSA Communist Party of South Africa – multi-racial, founded in 1921 and reformed in 1953 as the SACP (see below)

FNLA National Front for the Liberation of Angola – weakest of the three conflicting Angolan liberation movements, active in the 1970s

FRELIMO Front for the Liberation of Mozambique – took over from the Portuguese in 1974

FSAW Federation of South African Women – multi-racial women's movement active in the 1950s

ICU Industrial and Commercial Workers' Union – an early, huge black trade union movement, active for a short period in the 1920s

INKATHA – a Zulu political party violently against the ANC in the 1980s and 1990s. Originally, in the 1920s, a Zulu cultural movement

MK Umkhonto we Sizwe (Spear of the People) – terrorist wing of the ANC set up after the Sharpeville massacre of 1960

MPLA Popular Front for the Liberation of Angola – communist-backed and strongest of the three Angolan liberation movements. Became the Angolan government after the Portuguese left in 1974

NP National Party – the white, mainly Afrikaner political party which ruled South Africa from 1948 to 1994

NUSAS National Union of South African Students – the mainly white students' organisation

OAU Organisation of African Unity – set up in 1963, its members were the independent black nations of Africa

PAC Pan-African Congress – black political movement which split off from the ANC in 1959

PFP Progressive Federal Party – white, liberal, the main parliamentary opposition to the National Party in the 1970s and 1980s

Poqo (We go it alone) – the terrorist wing of the PAC

RENAMO – anti-FRELIMO (see above) movement in Mozambique, supported by the white South African government

SADF South African Defence Force – the South African army

SANNC South African Native National Congress (see ANC above)

SACP South African Communist Party (see CPSA above)

SASO South African Students' Organisation – set up by black students for black students in 1969. Steve Biko was its first president

SWAPO South-West African People's Organisation – successful black liberation movement in Namibia (South West Africa)

UDF United Democratic Front – multi-racial organisation opposing P. W. Botha's National Party government in the 1980s

UDI Unilateral Declaration of Independence – in 1965 whites in Rhodesia (Zimbabwe) defied the British government and refused to agree to black majority rule

UN United Nations – international peace-keeping organisation set up in 1945 to which virtually every independent nation belongs

UNITA National Union for the Total Independence of Angola – the third of the competing black Angolan liberation movements, supported by the white South African government against the MPLA (see above)

UP United Party – the political party formed by Smuts and Hertzog in 1934.

ZANU Zimbabwean African National Union – the black liberation movement which won power in Zimbabwe (Rhodesia) in 1980

Important dates in South African history

The first inhabitants

About AD 1100	Khoisan spread across the country and black farmers settle in the east
1100–1700	The number of black farmers increases and settle more of the east and south coast as far as the Great Fish River
1652	The Dutch build a fort at Cape Town, beginning white settlement

Early racial conflict

1652–1770	Khoisan lose their lands and often their lives to whites through war and disease
1779	The first 'Frontier' war between the black and white farmers
1806	The British take the Cape from the Dutch
1835–41	Dutch farmers (Boers) travel into the interior to escape from British rule - the so-called 'Great Trek'
1790–1881	A series of white-against-black wars which end with whites taking virtually all the blacks' land

Rapid economic growth and war between the whites

1867	Diamonds discovered
1886	Gold discovered
1899–1902	War between the British and the Boers. The British victory leads to the whole of South Africa becoming a single country and part of the British Empire
1910	By the Act of Union, Britain hands over political power to South Africa's whites, of whom the Boers (Afrikaners) are the majority
1912	The first black national political party, the South African Native National Congress (SANNC) founded
1913	The Land Act allows only 7% of the country for the black majority
1914–18	South Africa fights with Britain against Germany and gains possession of South-West Africa (Namibia) under the supervision of the League of Nations

Segregation and the growth of black resistance

1923–1937	Segregation between the races increased by a series of laws passed by white governments
1920s and 1930s	Black opposition grows through trade unions like the ICU and political parties like the ANC
1939–1945	South Africa, with Jan Smuts as Prime Minister, again fights with Britain against Germany. Growing prosperity and movement of people from the countryside into the towns
1940–48	African National Congress, with its Youth League, grows stronger and clearer in its demands for greater political rights for the black majority

Early apartheid and peaceful protest

1948	Malan's National Party wins the 1948 general election, having promised 'apartheid' or greater separation between the races
1948–58	First phase of apartheid, Baaskap or 'white supremacy' with many racist laws passed
1952	Peaceful black protests increase. 'Defiance' campaign, eg burning passes, travelling in 'whites only' compartments, mass arrests and some deaths
1955	Multi-racial and democratic Freedom Charter signed at Kliptown by the main resistance groups
1956	Treason Trials. 156 of the most important anti-apartheid leaders arrested and put on trial

Verwoerd's apartheid leads to more violent resistance

1958	Verwoerd becomes Prime Minister. The second 'separate development' phase of apartheid
1960	The Sharpeville and Langa massacres Verwoerd bans the ANC Oliver Tambo sets up the ANC in exile
1961	Mandela goes 'underground' to organise MK and begins acts of sabotage
1962	Mandela arrested
1963	ANC and MK leaders arrested at Lilliesleaf Farm, Rivonia
1964	'Rivonia' Trial. ANC/MK leaders including Mandela sentenced to life imprisonment
1965	Whites in Rhodesia (Zimbabwe) rebel against the British government (UDI)
1966	Verwoerd murdered in Parliament, succeeded as Prime Minister by Vorster

	Black resistance grows in strength
1969	The Morogoro Conference gives new life to the ANC in exile
1970s	UN and OAU lead campaigns for economic sanctions and sporting boycotts against South Africa
1973–5	Black opposition within South Africa strengthens through trade union action and the Black Consciousness movement led by Steve Biko
1974–5	Independent black governments replace Portuguese in Angola and Mozambique
1976	The white government declares Transkei the first 'independent' Bantustan
1976	School pupils lead riots in Soweto
1970s and 1980s	Massive forced removals of black people from areas the government declared to be 'white'
	The overthrow of apartheid and the triumph of the ANC
1978	P. W. Botha replaces Vorster as Prime Minister
1980	An independent black government wins power in Zimbabwe (Rhodesia). SWAPO guerrillas fight with increasing success in South-West Africa (Namibia) ANC guerrillas active within South Africa
1980s	Botha's government makes some reforms but unrest in the townships grows
1985	State of emergency declared because of serious rioting in the townships. Black resistance makes many parts of the country ungovernable. Economic crisis as more economic sanctions are imposed and major international businesses pull out of South Africa
1989	De Klerk replaces Botha as Prime Minister and declares the need for major changes SWAPO forms the black independent government of Namibia
1990	Mandela released from prison Serious continuing violence between ANC and Inkatha supporters, especially in KwaZulu/Natal
1992	CODESA discussions begin Boipatong and Bisho massacres
1993	Constitutional agreements reached
1994	First democratic election in South Africa's history is won by the ANC. Mandela becomes President
1996	National Party withdraws from Government of National Unity
1999	Mandela retires. Second democratic election is won by the ANC with an increased majority. Mbeki becomes President.

Index